Going to University

A Canadian Guide for Students
in Grades 9 to 12 and their Parents

BEVERLY CAMERON, PH.D.

GOING TO PRESS

Copyright © 1996 by Beverly Cameron

All rights reserved. This book may not be reproduced, in whole or in part, in any form or by any means electronic or mechanical, including photocopying, without permission from the publisher.

Printed in Canada

Cover and book designed by Barry Hammond, Flamingo Design, Winnipeg, Manitoba

Printed and bound by Kromar Printing Ltd., Winnipeg, Manitoba

Canadian Cataloguing in Publication Data

Cameron, Beverly J.

    Going to University : a Canadian guide for students in grades 9 to 12 and their parents

    Includes index.
    ISBN 0-9681420-0-1

1. College choice - Canada. 2. Universities and colleges - Canada - Admission. 3. Universities and colleges - United States - Admission. I. Title.

LB2350.5.C3 1996   378.1'05'0971   C96-920156-7

Published by: Going to Press
PO Box 23044, RPO McGillivray, Winnipeg, Manitoba R3T 5S3

Distributed in Canada by: Orca Book Publishers
PO Box 5626, Station B, Victoria, British Columbia V8R 6S4
1-800-210-5277 (604) 380-1229 fax (604) 380-1892 e-mail orca@pinc.com

Bulk orders of 20 or more copies may be purchased by schools and parents' associations at a 25% discount off the single copy price. Orders must be received by the distributor on official school or association letterhead to qualify for the discount.

The author wishes to thank the University of Manitoba Public Affairs office for permission to use the photos that appear in this book. Photos by Bob Tinker and Daniel Wexler.

This book is dedicated to my sons,

Ewen and Fraser,

whose educational aspirations

prompted me to search for the information

contained in these pages.

Contents

Acknowledgments	vii
Preface	viii
Chapter 1: Thinking About Going to University	2
Finding a Good Fit	3
Campus Cultures	3
Calculating the Costs and Benefits	6
Chapter 2: Planning Ahead and Starting Early	12
Chapter 3: Identifying Your Interests and Future Career Options	18
Chapter 4: Selecting a School that is Right for You	22
School Selection Questionnaire	23
I've Completed the Questionnaire! Now What?	27
Chapter 5: Published Sources of Information on Canadian Schools	32
Chapter 6: Published Sources of Information on American Schools	36
Chapter 7: University Information on the Internet	44
The Parent's Guide Home Page	46
Chapter 8: Information on CD-ROMs	48
Chapter 9: Looking for Scholarships and Financial Aid	52
Scholarships for Canadian Universities	53
Financial Aid for Canadian Universities	55

Scholarships and Financial Aid for American Universities	56
Athletic Scholarships in Particular	57
Chapter 10: Visiting Universities	60
How to Interview a School	62
Some Questions to Ask	63
Chapter 11: Applications and Admission Requirements	68
Canadian Universities	69
The Application Process	69
Admission Standards	71
American Colleges and Universities	71
Standardized Tests Used for Admissions	73
Chapter 12: Small Colleges within Large Universities	78
Chapter 13: Distance Education	82
Chapter 14: Leaving Home for University	86
Things to Take	89
Chapter 15: Other Educational Possibilities	94
Summer Opportunities for Grade 10 to 12 Students	94
Taking a Grade 13 Year Before University	98
A Final Thought	102
Index	104

Acknowledgments

This book is the result of the hard work, helpful suggestions, and encouragement of a number of people. Carole Marshall has contributed editorial comments, organizational skills and infectious enthusiasm for this project. Several parents, students, high school guidance counsellors, and university faculty members have reviewed and commented on the manuscript as it progressed: Carla Paler, Mya Brown, Linda Radcliffe, Holly and Paul McNally, George and Vijay Daniels, Kathy Brock, Linda Rzeszutek, Monica Lawrence, Maxine Chubaty and Fraser Cameron. Their comments have made this book more useful to students with a variety of educational goals and aspirations. Viola Prowse, Mitch McGuigan and Don and Evelyn Fletcher contributed resources to make this project a reality. Many others made valuable suggestions, provided information and contributed time and effort. My husband Norm Cameron read and commented on several drafts of the manuscript. The desktop publishing skills of Barry Hammond (Flamingo Design) have been invaluable. To all of you many thanks. This has truly been a team project.

Preface

Canadians' perceptions of their universities are changing. In the past, many people believed that the undergraduate experience at any one Canadian university was interchangeable with the experience at all or most other Canadian universities. It was common to hear, "It doesn't matter where you do your undergraduate work." As a result, most students attended the university closest to their home without investigating options at other schools.

In the last few years, however, federal and provincial budget cutbacks have started to change university offerings significantly. Today, most schools cannot afford to offer the wide range of programs, degree options, and extracurricular activities that they once did. Whole programs have been cut or shrunk; others have been amalgamated into joint offerings with nearby schools. Universities are redefining their mission statements and objectives, carving out niches to differentiate themselves, doing fewer things in order to do those things well, and building centres of excellence.

The ranking of universities by *Maclean's* has also served to differentiate schools in people's minds. *Maclean's* rankings, although often criticized by university administrators, have become widely quoted and eagerly awaited by many members of the public. *Maclean's* has become part of the discussion of higher education in Canada.

Most Canadian students prefer to stay in Canada for their university education, but some want to consider possibilities in the United States and elsewhere. For students who want to consider other possibilities, this book contains basic information and lists of information sources for students who are curious about universities in the United States.

Rising tuition and other costs associated with a university education, the increasing popularity of distance education, and discussions of privatizing some universities have prompted many Canadians to re-examine the university experience. All of these pressures are causing students and their parents to look more widely and more carefully at their options for a university education. This book is designed to help them look by: (1) providing some basic information about Canadian and American universities, (2) suggesting questions that students will need to find answers to as they make decisions about universities, and (3) making suggestions on how students, their parents, and high school guidance counsellors can find the information to answer these questions.

GOING TO UNIVERSITY

Thinking About Going to University

Whether and where to go to university are decisions that will have a large effect on the rest of your life, your educational and social experiences, your network of friends and colleagues, your options for professional and graduate schools, and your familiarity with various parts of Canada and the world. Going to university is one of the important decisions that you'll make in your life. You want the experience to be as rewarding and productive as possible.

FINDING A GOOD FIT

Each fall, many students start their university careers with a great deal of enthusiasm and motivation, only to drop out - discouraged - somewhere between then and the start of their second year. This isn't always because the students didn't put a great deal of effort into their studies, or because the school that they were attending wasn't a 'good' university. They may have dropped out because there wasn't a good fit between the student and the school.

Students sometimes select a school because their friends are going there, because their parents went there, or for other reasons unrelated to their own educational and personal needs. A student who might flourish in a small friendly school where most students know each other can become discouraged and alienated by a large commuter campus where it's harder to make friends. A student who can thrive in a large cosmopolitan urban university might feel stifled in a small school with more limited entertainment, athletic, or inter-cultural opportunities. A student who feels alienated and alone in a large university might have a very positive experience in a small college associated with that same large university. (e.g., Huron College in the University of Western Ontario, St. John's College in the University of Manitoba. See page 78.) A great deal of time, effort and money can be wasted when a poor fit occurs, but this doesn't have to happen. Forethought and planning will increase the chances of a good fit.

CAMPUS CULTURES

The culture on a university campus is hard to define in words, but it can make a big difference to whether there is a good fit between a particular student and a school. You can usually sense a campus culture after a few days. It is a combination of pride in the institution, school spirit, student attendance at athletic events, the attitude and friendliness of faculty and staff to students, student attitudes towards learning and grades, alumni support and involvement, friendliness of upper level students to first year students, the level of student participation in clubs, how much time students spend on campus each week, what time of day most students leave the campus, the amount of participation in intramural athletics, traditions that are passed on to entering students, the prominence of student government, weekend social events, and many other attitudes and behaviours that are hard to measure.

Commuter and Residential Campuses

For example, the University of Calgary is essentially a commuter school where most of the 16,000 undergraduate students drive to campus for classes and leave soon after. Few students attend intercollegiate athletic events, and there is little school spirit in the 'rah rah' sense, but students are proud of their school. Politically, U of C students tend to be conservative, but there are frequent debates on social and economic issues.

Acadia University in Wolfville, Nova Scotia has a quite different campus culture. With just over 4,000 students in a town of 3,500, Acadia has more emphasis on social events within its ivy-covered red brick campus. Athletics events are well attended by students, and Acadia sweatshirts are frequently seen on campus. The University is small enough that there is a real sense of community. People are treated as individuals, but some students say Acadia can be cliquish.

Queen's University in Kingston, Ontario is a residential campus of just over 13,000 students where most students live on or within a mile of the campus. Queen's is highly selective in its admissions, and Queen's students, by and large, love their university and are very proud of it. Students are said to work hard, and play hard. The academic environment at Queen's is competitive, and the weekend social life plentiful.

The University of British Columbia's (UBC) culture is similar to Queen's in some ways, and quite different in others. UBC also has a selective admissions policy, but it is more than twice the size of Queen's with a total enrollment of over 30,000 students. The campus spirit of Queen's is hard to find at UBC since so many students live elsewhere and commute in for classes. Students can feel a bit alienated and overwhelmed by the size of UBC, and they have to take the initiative to become involved in clubs and organizations. When students get involved, their feelings toward UBC become much warmer.

These examples not only contrast schools of different sizes, they also contrast commuter campuses with residential campuses. When the main focus of students' social lives is on campus, as it is for largely residential campuses like Acadia and Queen's, the campus culture is greatly enriched.

Other Influences on Campus Culture

Special programs, student organizations, and support for certain groups of students can influence the campus culture for individual students. For example, Aboriginal students may feel particularly at home because of the special services and support networks offered to them at schools such as Brandon University, the Universities of Manitoba, Saskatchewan, Toronto, Northern British Columbia and McMaster University. Schools may also have special support networks for adult, single-parent and disabled students.

The campus cultures at new universities such as Royal Roads University in Victoria and the University of Northern British Columbia in Prince George will also be different than those at older established schools like McGill in Montreal and Saint Francis Xavier in Antigonish, Nova Scotia. Royal Roads and UNBC are establishing their identities and traditions, while McGill and St. F. X. have already been shaped by their long histories.

Campus culture is also influenced by shared religious beliefs. For example, the culture at Augustana University College in Camrose, Alberta, reflects its affiliation with the Evangelical Lutheran Church, and the culture at Redeemer College in Ancaster, Ontario, is influenced by its Christian heritage.

Campus cultures are unique. What one student might see as a positive attribute, another might see as a drawback. The goal is for each student to find a school and a campus culture that is the right fit for him or her.

CALCULATING THE COSTS AND BENEFITS

Like many good things, a university experience isn't without its costs. Going to university involves a sizable financial commitment. At the very least, you'll need extra money for tuition and books. Based on 1996 totals for tuition and fees at Canadian universities, you'll be out of pocket between $2,200 and $4,500, and with continuing government cutbacks these fees are likely to continue to increase. Required books, computer disks, calculators, CD-ROMs and other supplies will add another $400 to $900.

What the other costs of going to university are depends on what you would have done otherwise. If you would have worked full-time after high school if you hadn't gone to university, the salary you won't be earning is an extra cost of going to university. If you would have lived at home, and going to university requires moving into an apartment, the increased expenses of the apartment are an extra cost of going to university. However, if you would have moved into an apartment anyway, had you gone to university or not, the apartment costs are not an extra cost of going to university. And if you would have traveled the world on a shoestring budget, then you forego the world experience, but save the shoestring by going to university instead.

Here is a 4-step process that will leave you with a proper measure of the net extra cost of going to university - a measure economists call the opportunity cost.

(1) **Add up** all the expenses for tuition, books, room and board, entertainment, transportation, and so on, that you can foresee for a year at university.

(2) **Subtract** any scholarship, bursary, or other income you would receive as a university student.

It can cost a student as little as $1,900 more to live away from home than to live at home.

(3) Subtract all the expenses you would have had in your most likely alternative use of the year.

(4) Add any income you gave up earning by going to university instead.

The result is the net extra cost of going to university for that year.

Table 1 provides an example for a student who leaves home to go to university, who works part time and has a scholarship, but who would have held a full-time job and lived at home if he or she hadn't gone to university. If your situation fits the example in Table 1, the extra cost of a year at university is $20,500. In this figure, the biggest item is the foregone wages of $20,000 that you would have earned if you were working full time. However, the $20,000 cost is partly offset by part-time work while at university.

Notice in the example in Table 1 that the living expenses from leaving home to go to university (the last three items in part (1) which total $8,600) are not much different from the living expenses of staying at home (the same three items in part (3) which total $6,700). In Table 1, the extra cost of leaving home is only $1,900 (= $8,600 - $6,700). This is only an example, but it is much less than many people expect.

Students and parents often think that it's much more expensive to go away to university because they don't recognize all the costs of a student living at home. The costs of living at home include food bills, entertainment costs, wear and tear on the car, water and electricity use, wear and tear on the appliances, heating, telephone and possibly other expenses peculiar to each student. These are the extra costs that wouldn't exist if the student wasn't living at home. Parents may not calculate these expenses as costs of going to university, because they are easily folded into the overall household expenses. However, living at home is never free; having one less person in the house does significantly reduce household expenses. In this example the cost of living at home for a year is estimated at $6,700. Your own estimate may not be much different.

TABLE 1: THE COST OF A YEAR AT UNIVERSITY: AN EXAMPLE

(1) Add expenses while at university

tuition	$3,400
books and supplies	$700
room and board (in a residence or apartment)	$7,000
transportation	$600
entertainment and other costs	$1,000
Total	**$12,700**

(2) Subtract any income received at university

scholarships	$2,500
part-time job	$3,000
Total	**$5,500**

(3) Subtract expenses of living where you would otherwise have lived if you hadn't gone to university

room and board at home (your share of food, extra utilities and other extra household expenses)	$5,300
transportation costs	$400
entertainment and other costs	$1,000
Total	**$6,700**

(4) Add any wages you would otherwise have earned

Full-time wages with Grade 12 education	$20,000

Equals

The extra cost of the year at university	**$20,500**

The examples used in Table 1 may not fit your circumstances, but the 4-step calculation process which it illustrates does fit everyone.

As high as these costs may seem, these Canadian figures are low compared to the $14,000US to $28,000US you'll pay for room, board and tuition at many schools in the United States. Any way you look at it, going to university is costly.

However, a university education is probably the best investment you'll ever make. Labour force data shows that individuals with university degrees are much less likely to be unemployed. (See Chart 1.) Employers continue to look for individuals with well developed analytical and problem-solving skills; and the rapidly changing economy requires educated and mentally-flexible individuals who can adapt to new situations. (See Table 2.) The message in this book is not that you should become discouraged at the cost of going to university; it is that you should ask some questions before you commit your time, money and energy to any one university program.

> *A university education is probably the best investment you'll ever make.*

CHART 1: AVERAGE UNEMPLOYMENT RATES IN CANADA BY EDUCATIONAL ATTAINMENT 1989-1994*

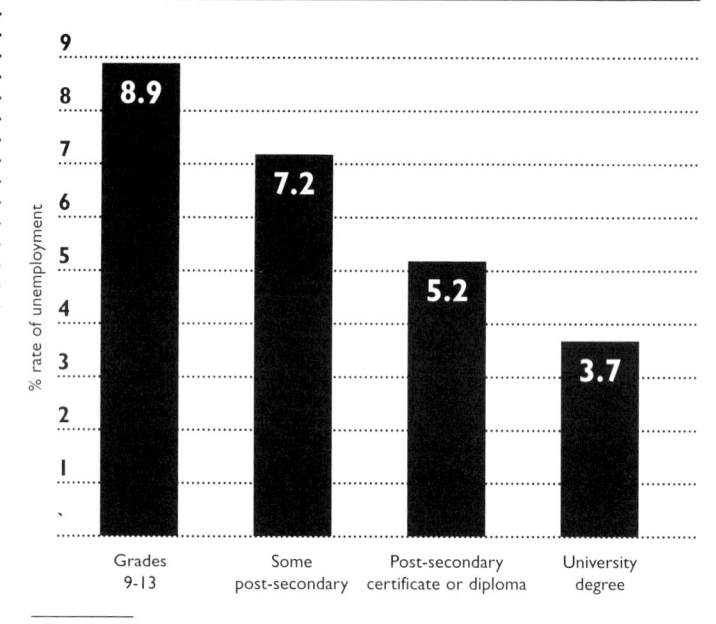

Educational Attainment	% rate of unemployment
Grades 9-13	8.9
Some post-secondary	7.2
Post-secondary certificate or diploma	5.2
University degree	3.7

Source: Statistics Canada Labour Force Survey

*1989 to 1994 was a recessionary period in Canada with slow economic growth, government cutbacks and corporate downsizing.

TABLE 2: EDUCATION AND TRAINING REQUIREMENTS

Years of education/training	1995 Labour Force Requirements	1995-2000 New Job Requirements
Less than 12 years	45.4%	44.7%
12 years	7.7%	3.0%
13-16 years	20.9%	10.6%
17 or more years	26.0%	41.7%

Source: Human Resource Development Canada. Canadian Occupational Projection System (COPS), 1996

GOING TO UNIVERSITY

Planning Ahead and Starting Early

If you're considering university after Grade 12, it's best to start thinking about your options by Grade 10. Starting early is especially important if you're considering an American college or university because of their slightly different admission criteria. (See page 71.) Just as in preparing for an important test or exam, cramming all your university planning into the fall of your Grade 12 year will not leave you as satisfied as small amounts of planning spread over several years. Part of the planning is for you to identify what kind of university you should be looking for, and that identification process can take a lot of time and thought.

Here is a timetable that will leave you well prepared and informed by the time you start sending out university applications in Grade 12.

Grades 9 & 10 (Senior 1 & 2)

- Think about why you might want to go to university.
- Talk to parents and teachers about your interests and goals.
- Assess your personal and academic strengths.
- Talk to university students about their experiences.
- Look through a university guide book or calendar to see what they contain.
- Attend a presentation by a university representative at your school.
- Visit a university campus, just to look around.
- Plan some extracurricular, volunteer, and work experiences for the next few years. These activities will help you think about what you want from university studies, and having them on your resume will give you an edge in getting accepted to highly selective schools. These experiences can also give you valuable insights for future career choices.

Also, if you're interested in American schools:

- Remember that American colleges and universities look at your grades starting from Grade 9 when they consider you for admission. (Don't wait until Grade 11 to start working harder.)
- You can take the Preliminary Scholastic Assessment Test (PSAT) in Grade 10, and you may want to do this as practice for the SAT. (See page 74.)
- Consider taking the Scholastic Assessment Test II (SAT II) achievement tests in subjects you plan to discontinue. e.g., French.** (See page 75.)

Grade 11 (Senior 3)

- Consult university handbooks, and meet with university representatives when they visit your high school.

**Some US colleges and universities require proficiency in a language other than English as a graduation requirement. Many Canadian students are able to fill this requirement with French. A suffiently high score on the French SAT II Achievement Test taken at the point where the student elects to stop French classes - possibly at the end of grade 10 - may fill this requirement.

- Get information on university course and program offerings, costs, enrollments, locations, admission requirements, and application deadlines.
- Ask your guidance counsellor about scholarships you might be eligible to receive.
- Visit two or three universities with your parents - maybe on a summer or winter holiday trip - to help you narrow your choices.
- Ask your guidance counsellor if you can take an interest inventory to help you think about what you may want to pursue in university. (e.g., Myers-Briggs Type Indicator®, Strong Interest Inventory™) (See page 19.)
- Plan your Grade 12 courses to make sure that you meet university entrance requirements in your areas of interest. (e.g., computer science, calculus)

Also, if you're considering American schools:
- Take the PSAT and discuss the results with your parents and college counsellor. (See page 74.)
- Prepare for and register to take the SAT I and SAT II in May or June if you would like early admission decisions. (See page 75.)

Grade 12 (Senior 4)
September to January
- Talk to your parents and meet with your guidance counsellor if you're considering large changes in your university plans.
- Attend presentations by all universities that visit your high school even if you're only remotely considering the school. You could change your mind or get some other valuable information about the schools you are more interested in.
- Get university and scholarship applications forms from your guidance counsellor and write for those you do not have.
- Check on application and scholarship deadlines and prepare for them well in advance so you can present yourself as well as possible.
- Apply for scholarships that you may be eligible to receive. Apply even if you think your chances are slim. If you don't apply, you definitely won't get a scholarship, and some have few applicants.

Apply for scholarships even if you think your chances are slim.

- Arrange campus visits for two or three schools you are seriously considering.
- Talk to students from your school who are attending universities to which you're applying. Remember that students in their second or third year may have a more informed view of university life than those in their first year. You may learn some valuable information about which residence to ask for, how to get all the classes you want, which professors are best, and so on.
- Encourage your parents to talk to the parents of students who are attending universities to which you're applying if they, or you, have any questions - or even if you don't.
- Get financial aid information.

December to February

- Send applications to all universities in which you have an interest.
- Although Canadian schools do not require the SAT or ACT (See page 74.), if you have taken these tests you may want to send your scores to Canadian schools to give them additional information about your abilities.
- Request that your high school send copies of your official transcript to all the schools to which you have applied.
- Ask high school teachers and others to write reference letters required for your applications.

March to June

- Notify your high school of university acceptances, so they can send your final transcript after June graduation.

Also, if you're applying to American schools:

August

- Prepare for and register to take or retake the ACT or SAT I and SAT II for October/November. (See page 74.)

October and November

- Submit applications by October or November deadlines if you want an early decision or special scholarship consideration. Regular application

Planning ahead and starting early will help you make the best decision.

deadlines are often in January, so check on the individual school deadlines.

November to January
- Make sure your SAT or ACT scores are sent to all American schools to which you apply.
- Send all remaining applications, being sure to meet deadlines.

December
- Ask your parents to complete United States financial aid forms if you want financial help.

GOING TO UNIVERSITY

Identifying Your Interests and Future Career Options

High school is a time to think about and explore future career directions. In addition to traditional careers and professions, the changing world economy is creating new possibilities on a weekly basis. This means that many students' career options are limited only by their imaginations. While this range of possibilities and options is exciting, it can also be confusing and a bit frightening. The right career choice, like selecting the right school, is not something that is likely to jump out at you overnight. Here are some suggestions that may give you some ideas and help you make choices.

- Look at the career choices made by family members and friends. Ask them these questions: Are they pleased with their choices? Would they change their decision if they could make the choice again? Would they advise you to choose the same career? Have their career decisions allowed them to enjoy the life-style they had hoped for? Where would they choose to get their university education if they were starting over today? What do they think the future is for their career or profession? Finally, if their career still seems like a possibility for you, ask if you could spend a day or more on the job with them to get a better idea of what the job involves.
- Talk to your high school guidance counsellor or a professional career counsellor about career options that are open to you. Your counsellor may suggest that you take one of several interest inventories which are available to help people make career choices. Four of the more popular inventories are:

   1) The Myers-Briggs Type Indicator® (MBTI) is a widely used personality preference inventory to help individuals make important personal and career choices. The MBTI is a reliable tool which is administered yearly to millions of people around the world. The 126 item MBTI takes about a half hour to complete. When you finish, your counsellor will discuss the results with you, and describe career choices that others with preferences similar to yours have chosen. The MBTI will give you valuable insights into yourself and may open possibilities you had not considered.

   2) The Strong Interest Inventory™ measures a student's interest in a broad range of school subjects, leisure activities and occupations. The *Strong Interest Inventory* reflects today's changing work world and provides a useful guide for career choice decisions. The inventory uses 317 items to determine career interests, and includes a profile snapshot of the results.

   3) Choices is a career guidance package that is available on CD-ROM or disk through guidance counsellors. *Choices* uses your responses to questions to make suggestions on career paths you might want to consider.

4) The *ACT Interest Inventory* measures student interests in six different dimensions, and the results are compared with the interests of university students who later select certain majors. The Inventory results help students compare their preferences for work activities to the activities required by certain career groups. Information on the *ACT Interest Inventory* can be obtained from the ACT National Office. (See page 74.)

- Read newspapers and magazines with an eye for interesting career options and possibilities. Many publications print profiles of successful individuals in a variety of careers. If some of those careers sound interesting to you, note the education, training, and job experiences that led these individuals to their careers.
- Read career advertisement sections of major newspapers such as the *Globe and Mail* to learn about current jobs and to get a feel for trends in business, government, and education. Reading job descriptions, and the qualifications requested of applicants, can give you ideas for shaping your educational and career plans.
- Go to a book store or library and look at career guides. One interesting guide is *Do What You Are: Discover the Perfect Career for You Through the Secrets of Personality Type*, by Paul Tieger and Barbara Barron-Tieger. This book is based on the Myers-Briggs Type Indicator® and provides some interesting career-related profiles for each MBTI type. If you'd like to explore the Myers-Briggs career-related literature on your own, a shortened version of the MBTI can be found in *Please Understand Me* by David Keirsey and Marilyn Bates.
- Students may want to enter a general university program and wait until they have completed a year of studies before exploring career options. Most universities provide excellent counseling services to help students explore career possibilities.

GOING TO UNIVERSITY

Selecting a School that is Right for You

More than 50 universities grant undergraduate degrees in Canada. More than 1000 colleges and universities do so in the United States. Each school has its own strengths and weaknesses, each has a slightly different educational philosophy or mission, and each campus has its own special culture. (See page 3.) It takes some looking to find the school where you can meet your educational goals, enjoy being intellectually challenged by your professors and classmates, meet friends and future professional colleagues, and feel comfortable socially.

Every school isn't right for every student, because every student is different and every school is different. However, with a little planning and effort you'll find a match that will allow you to look back on your university days as some of the best years of your life.

SCHOOL SELECTION QUESTIONNAIRE

How do you select a university? You start by identifying as clearly as possible what features you are looking for in a university. Then you can compare universities on all of those features, so you'll be ready to make an informed choice when it comes time to send in applications. The questionnaire that follows will help you with the selection process.

	YES	UNSURE	NO

Location

1. I prefer to stay in the city where I currently live. ❑ ❑ ❑
2. I prefer to stay in my home province. ❑ ❑ ❑
3. I prefer to live in another part of Canada for university. ❑ ❑ ❑
4. I want to attend an American or other non-Canadian school. ❑ ❑ ❑
5. I'd like to be in a large city. ❑ ❑ ❑
6. I'd like to be in a small or medium-size city. ❑ ❑ ❑
7. I'd like to be in a small town or rural area. ❑ ❑ ❑
8. Given my academic and career interests (e.g., art, drama, music, politics, business) an urban setting could offer me more opportunities and experiences. ❑ ❑ ❑
9. Given my academic and career interests (e.g., agriculture, environmental studies, outdoor

	YES	UNSURE	NO

recreation) a rural or small city setting could offer me more opportunities and experiences. ❏ ❏ ❏

10. Given my current situation I do not want to have to attend classes at regular times. ❏ ❏ ❏

University Size

11. It's important for me to be in a small school, or a small college within a larger university, where I will know most or all of my classmates. ❏ ❏ ❏

12. It's important for me to be in a larger school where I can meet many new people with differing interests. ❏ ❏ ❏

13. I prefer to have mostly small classes. (e.g., 40 and fewer) ❏ ❏ ❏

14. I prefer a small school where I am likely to get more personalized attention from professors. ❏ ❏ ❏

	YES	UNSURE	NO

15. I prefer a combination of large and small classes. (e.g., some classes of 100 or more) ❏ ❏ ❏

Student Characteristics and Campus Life

16. I prefer to be with students who come mainly from my geographic area. ❏ ❏ ❏

17. I prefer to be with students who come from a variety of geographic areas of Canada and/or the world. ❏ ❏ ❏

18. I would prefer that most students share my religious affiliation. ❏ ❏ ❏

19. I prefer a single-sex school. ❏ ❏ ❏

20. I prefer a school where most students live in residence or within a mile of campus. ❏ ❏ ❏

21. I prefer a commuter campus where most students live off campus and come in for classes. ❏ ❏ ❏

	YES	UNSURE	NO

22. I prefer a school with an active campus life during the week. ❏ ❏ ❏

23. I prefer a school where most students stay on campus for the weekends and there is an active weekend campus life. ❏ ❏ ❏

Sports and Extracurricular Activities

24. I would like to participate in a specific intercollegiate sports team, and want a school that fields a team in that sport. ❏ ❏ ❏

25. I would like a school with a wide range of intramural sports teams with high levels of student participation. ❏ ❏ ❏

26. I would prefer a school with active student government organizations in which I might participate. ❏ ❏ ❏

27. It is important to me to have a wide range of student clubs in which I could participate. ❏ ❏ ❏

	YES	UNSURE	NO

Educational Mission

28. I would prefer a school whose main mission is excellence in undergraduate teaching. ❏ ❏ ❏

29. I would prefer a school that has a wide range of graduate and research programs as well as undergraduate programs. ❏ ❏ ❏

30. I prefer a school that has a wide range of courses and degree programs. ❏ ❏ ❏

31. I prefer a school that specializes in a few areas and courses of study. (e.g., music, engineering) ❏ ❏ ❏

32. I would like a school with innovative programs, opportunities for study abroad, exchange programs, a range of courses on the Internet, a well developed distance education program, and so on. ❏ ❏ ❏

	YES	UNSURE	NO
33. I prefer a traditional school with relatively fixed degree requirements.	❏	❏	❏
34. I want a 3 year degree as opposed to a 4 year or longer degree program.	❏	❏	❏
35. I want a school that has professional schools in addition to basic arts and science programs.	❏	❏	❏

Academic Environment

	YES	UNSURE	NO
36. I prefer a selective or highly selective school where all my peers will have academic abilities similar to mine.	❏	❏	❏
37. I prefer a somewhat selective school with peers who have a range of academic abilities.	❏	❏	❏
38. I prefer an open admission school where my peers will have a very wide range of academic backgrounds and abilities.	❏	❏	❏

	YES	UNSURE	NO
39. I prefer a school where most undergraduates are in the traditional age range of 18-22.	❏	❏	❏
40. I prefer a school where the undergraduate population spans a wide range of ages.	❏	❏	❏
41. I prefer a school where the latest technology is readily available to students.	❏	❏	❏

Financial Aid

	YES	UNSURE	NO
42. I will require some scholarship or financial aid.	❏	❏	❏
43. I'll need a part-time job while I'm in school.	❏	❏	❏

Co-op Programs

	YES	UNSURE	NO
44. I would like to participate in a co-op program.	❏	❏	❏

	YES	UNSURE	NO

Other

45. I prefer a school that will give me credit for Advanced Placement (AP) courses I complete in high school. ❑ ❑ ❑

46. I prefer a school that provides special support or programming for Aboriginal, single-parent, adult, or disabled students. ❑ ❑ ❑

47. I prefer a school that has a strong national and/or international reputation for its research and/or teaching. ❑ ❑ ❑

48. I prefer a French speaking or bilingual university. ❑ ❑ ❑

49. I prefer a school located in a mild climate with little or no winter. ❑ ❑ ❑

50. List any other features that are important to you personally.

I'VE COMPLETED THE QUESTIONNAIRE! NOW WHAT?

Once you've answered these questions, use the grid on pages 29 and 30 to compare schools you're considering. First, go back and pick the 10 or 12 items from your 'yes' list that are the most important to you, and the 5 or 6 items from your 'unsure' list that you think you'd really like to consider further. Write these 15 to 18 items on the left side of your grid. List schools you've thought about, or have heard were interesting across the top of the grid. Then check off the characteristics each school has that are on your "yes" or "unsure" lists.

How do you find out if the schools on your list have the characteristics you value? This will take some work, some asking around, and for some questions, maybe even a campus visit. Your guidance counsellor, teachers, parents, university guides, university publications, the Internet, magazines, and friends who are now at university are all possible sources of information. The next few pages suggest some specific sources of the information you'll need.

This exercise will take some time and thought, but it will help you, at the very least, to narrow down the list of schools you want to check into more closely. The results may even indicate that you should look at schools you hadn't previously considered when you started this exercise. A very brief example of the selection grid that is suggested would look like the one below:

Your "yes" and "unsure" characteristics

	Queen's	U of Manitoba	Mt. Allison	UBC	McGill	U of Winnipeg	Trent University
prefer large city		x		x	x	x	
prefer a small school where I know most people			x			x	x
prefer mostly traditional-age student body	x		x				x
prefer a highly selective school	x			x	x		
prefer to stay in Manitoba		x				x	

GOING TO UNIVERSITY

Your "yes" and "unsure" characteristics

Your "yes" and "unsure" characteristics

GOING TO UNIVERSITY

Published Sources of Information on Canadian Schools

These are some of the more readily available published sources on Canadian colleges and universities. Your high school guidance counsellor may have most of these publications. If you have trouble finding any of these sources, check with library reference departments, in book stores, on magazine racks or with friends who went through the university selection process a year or two ago.

Library reference departments are a great free source of published information on universities.

1) ***The Real Guide to Canadian Universities***, edited by Sarah Borins, and published by Key Porter Books. This guide is written by students for students to tell you what it's like to be a student at 45 different Canadian schools from Acadia to York. It describes academic issues, academic facilities, how hard it is to get accepted, "residence reality," extracurricular activities, and gives "survival notes." *The Real Guide* is a fun read, costs about $25 and is available in many bookstores and libraries.

2) ***The Maclean's Guide to Universities: Profiles of 50 Schools plus Annual Rankings***. This guide first appeared in January 1996 and included the November 1995 *Maclean's* university rankings. The *Maclean's Guide* includes several articles on Canadian universities, descriptions of the schools, facts and figures, pictures, editorial comments, and a "campus confidential" section listing "what's hot, what's not, hot hangouts, 'bird' courses, popular profs, and famous grads." More information is given on schools that participate in the *Maclean's* rankings than on those that opt out. The 1996 edition sold for $9.95.

3) ***Maclean's Special Issue on Universities***. These special editions of *Maclean's* magazine have appeared in mid-November since 1991. Less complete than *Maclean's Guide to Universities*, the magazine includes several articles on Canadian universities plus the results of their annual rankings. Participating schools are ranked on a wide variety of categories within three separate groups: institutions that are primarily undergraduate schools, comprehensive universities, and institutions with medical schools and Ph.D. programs. Before you accept the ranking results, review *Maclean's* criteria and weightings to be sure your priorities for a school are the same as the editors'.

4) ***The Complete Guide to Canadian Universities: How to Select a University and Succeed When You Get There*** by Kevin Paul. This guide from Self-

Counsel Press contains information on university admission requirements and the application process, financing a university education, developing study skills and selecting a university that meets the needs of individual students. Universities offering co-op programs, correspondence degrees, and special services are listed. The *Complete Guide* also contains valuable information for international students and post-graduation job search skills. One page of basic information for each school and campus maps can be found at the end of the book. The *Complete Guide* is priced at $14.95.

5) ***Gourman Report: A Rating of Undergraduate Programs in American and International Universities.*** This annual report focuses on American schools and programs, but it does rank Canadian engineering programs. A second *Gourman Report* ranks graduate and professional programs in Canada (e.g., law, medical, dental and pharmacy schools), the U.S. and abroad. *Gourman Reports* are available at many library reference desks or for approximately $20US each from Dearborn Financial Publishing, 1-800-621-9621.

6) Writing directly to schools for information on their programs, admission requirements, campus life, and so on is also a good idea. You may want to make your first contact with a school by using e-mail or through the school's Internet home page. Most universities won't send you calendars because of the expense, but the information they will send free of charge is usually very informative and useful.

7) Your high school guidance counsellor should be a great source of information. He or she should be able to provide you with printed literature on schools, tell you the names of recent graduates from your school that have attended various universities, give you scholarship and admissions information, provide you with entrance requirements for various programs, and much more. Individual teachers in your high school may also have information about particular schools, so don't hesitate to ask.

GOING TO UNIVERSITY

Published Sources of Information on American Schools

As you look through the literature on American schools you'll notice references to colleges and universities, and you'll hear Americans talk about "going to college." Canadians tend to talk about "going to university," and use the term "college" to refer to community colleges or other institutions that do not offer bachelor's degrees.

In the United States, colleges are usually - but not always - four-year undergraduate schools that offer few or no graduate courses.

Universities in the U.S. usually offer both undergraduate and graduate degrees.

Most Canadian students are not interested in American schools because they prefer to stay in Canada. However, if you are interested in considering American schools the following books are some of the more readily available information sources. Bookstores in the United States often stock several college guides, but you may find it necessary to special order American guides in Canada. Your library may have some of these publications, but they may or may not be up to date.

The list below is certainly not an exhaustive one, but it does include many of the standard guides that students, parents and guidance counsellors have relied upon for years. New college and university guides appear frequently, so you may want to check newsstands and bookstores periodically.

1) **Barron's Guide to The Best, Most Popular, and Most Exciting Colleges** and **Barron's Guide to The Most Prestigious Colleges**. (Published by Barron's Educational Series, Inc.) Both books provide factual information on hundreds of colleges and universities. Undergraduate and graduate enrollment totals, number of men and women, number of international students, tuition, room and board costs, average test scores (e.g., SAT and ACT) for those admitted, application deadline and admission requirements, descriptions of the campus environment, student life, activities, sports, services, programs of study, special degree requirements, and financial aid possibilities are all included. The information is presented with little or no editorial comment.

2) *The Fiske Guide to Colleges*, by Edward B. Fiske, education columnist for *The New York Times*. (Published by Random House Times Books.) This very entertaining guide provides facts on enrollment, costs, financial aid, location, and percentage of applicants accepted and percentage of those accepted who enroll. In addition, it rates the quality of student life and social atmosphere with a star system in much the way hotels are rated. Best are the editorial comments on campus life and quotes from students on what it's like to attend each school.

PUBLISHED SOURCES OF INFORMATION ON AMERICAN SCHOOLS

3) *Lovejoy's College Guide*, edited by Charles T. Straughn II and Barbarasue Lovejoy Straughn. (Published by Macmillan, U.S.A.) Lovejoy's lists all the usual factual information and includes lists of schools that offer various programs. (e.g., child development studies, horticulture, languages-Slavic, entrepreneurial/small business management, glass science) Schools are also listed by special features such as: early-decision admission, guaranteed tuition programs, availability of kosher meals, schools on quarter or trimester systems, and so on. An introductory section on admission requirements for American schools is also helpful.

4) *Peterson's Four Year Colleges* provides the usual factual information on schools listed by state as well as two pages of more individualized information on each school. A special section lists schools by what majors are offered. This makes it possible to see at a glance the schools that offer unique majors such as equestrian studies, fashion merchandising, peace studies, plastics technology, tourism and travel, and wildlife biology, as well as the more conventional majors. The 1996 edition comes with a computer disk to help you plan your applications, a magazine on college life, and details on computer requirements and facilities at various schools. Peterson's also publishes regional college guides with the same kind of information but no computer disk or college-life magazine. (e.g., *Peterson's Guide to New England Colleges*)

5) *Princeton Review's Student Access Guide to the Best Colleges* by Tom Meltzer, Zachary Knower, Edward Custard, and John Katzman. This book rates itself as "the buyer's guide to colleges." In addition to the usual factual information on enrollments, application deadlines, financial aid, and tuition fees, this guide contains the results of student ratings on faculty accessibility, workload, class size, social life and sports. The guide also includes a list of independent American college counsellors with their addresses and phone numbers, and an

New college and university guides appear frequently, so check bookstores and newsstands periodically.

index of programs for the learning disabled offered by numerous schools. Written with editorial pizzazz, this guide tries to provide the flavour of each campus in two well laid out pages. Internet home page addresses are given for most schools.

6) *U.S. News and World Report Exclusive Rankings of the Best Colleges.* This annual publication has become an American institution. Published each fall, it contains useful articles on a variety of topics. Rankings are by geographic region of the U.S., as well as overall rankings for universities and liberal arts colleges that draw students from all over the U.S. Institutions are also ranked by financial soundness and other interesting characteristics and facts. E.g., In 1994, schools were ranked by the number of women they graduated between 1976 and 1981 who went on to earn Ph.D.'s in the life and physical sciences between 1981 and 1991. Before you accept the ranking results, review the *U.S. News* criteria and weightings to be sure your priorities for a school are the same as the editors'. *U.S. News* also publishes a "Best Colleges" insert in its September issue that looks at 500 colleges and universities.

7) *The Best College for You* is a new effort between *Time* magazine, the *Princeton Review* (See #5 above.) and *Apply* software. (See page 72.) *The Best College for You* includes a guide to help students match themselves with colleges and universities, and a CD-ROM to help students prepare multiple college applications. This guide is available on U.S. newsstands for $5.95US.

8) *How to Get Into College* is a new guide published in the fall by *Newsweek* magazine and Kaplan Educational Centers. (See page 73.) Information is provided on more than 1000 American schools. This guide is available on U.S. newsstands in the fall for $5.95US.

9) *Money* magazine publishes an insert in its September issue titled *"Your Best College Buys Now."* The top American colleges and universities are ranked according to "best value" for your education dollar.

10) *Gourman Report: A Rating of Undergraduate Programs in American and International Universities.* This annual report from National Education Standards in Los Angeles ranks numerous American schools by discipline and professional programs (e.g., engineering) according to stated criteria. In addition, rankings are made for the top 50 American undergraduate schools, university administrations, intercollegiate athletic programs, and other categories. Rankings for non-North American universities are also given. A second *Gourman Report* ranks graduate and professional programs in the U.S., Canada and abroad. Before you accept the ranking results, review Gourman's criteria to be sure your priorities for a school are the same as his. (See page 34.)

American guides with a more specialized focus include:

11) *Women's Colleges* by Joe Anne Adler with Jennifer Adler Friedman is a guide to 77 women's colleges. The guide includes a wide array of facts and figures, useful information on the admissions process, campus life, and more.

12) *The Performing Arts Major's College Guide* by Carole J. Everett is designed specifically for dance, drama, and music majors. This guide profiles the best performing arts programs at colleges and conservatories worldwide, provides expert advice on admissions, and gives general information for performing arts students.

13) *The Art Student's College Guide* by Carol Brown and Linda Sweetoe provides information on hundreds of visual arts programs at colleges, private schools, and vocational art schools. The guide profiles 225 top visual arts programs and includes information on course offerings, tuition, financial aid, and much more.

14) *Lovejoy's College Guide for the Learning Disabled* by Charles T. Straughn II provides essential information to allow learning disabled students to make the right choice of colleges. The guide profiles more than 270 colleges and universities that offer support services to learning disabled students.

15) ***The Transfer Student's Guide to Changing Colleges*** by Sidonia Dalby and Sally Rubenstone is a valuable guide for students who choose to transfer from one school to another during their university career. Advice, tips, and facts are provided by admissions officers who have had extensive experience helping students make successful transfers.

16) ***Historically Black Colleges and Universities*** published by Wintergreen/Orchard House, Inc. provides detailed information on all 84 accredited four-year historically black schools in the U.S. The guide is full of useful facts and figures, admissions information, and descriptions of campus life.

17) ***100 Colleges Where Average Students Can Excel*** by Joe Anne Adler provides valuable information on 100 top quality schools known for their innovative teaching, unique curricula, small class size, on-campus housing and much more. This guide is specifically for students who want a quality education but who may need extra help to attain it.

18) ***Colleges that Change Lives: 40 Schools You Should Know About Even If You're Not A Straight-A Student*** by Loren Pope profiles 40 small colleges that are known for their excellent academic programs, successful graduates, sense of community, emphasis on teaching, and the accessibility of faculty to students. The author builds a strong case for the rich educational experience offered at these lesser known schools with enrollments of fewer than 5000 students.

In addition, you can get information on American colleges and universities from the schools themselves or from your high school guidance counsellor.

GOING TO UNIVERSITY

University Information on the Internet

A great deal of university information is available on the Internet, and more schools are adding home pages every week. Home pages usually contain general and detailed information about the school, pictures of the campus, messages from presidents and various campus organizations, admission procedures, information on campus visits, maps of the campus, phone and e-mail directories, lists of faculty, and sometimes even the calendar and course outlines. University home pages may also link to pages written by various departments and individual professors.

Inside home pages you usually just click on highlighted words or an icon to get more information.

Many university home pages have a feature that allows you to send e-mail messages requesting application and admission information. This is a fast and inexpensive way to get many of your questions answered. Other schools allow you to fill out an application form and mail it electronically through their Internet sites.

Many university home pages let you send e-mail messages directly to admissions offices.

Canadian university home page Internet addresses generally follow this pattern:

http://www.ubc.ca/ for the University of British Columbia in Vancouver

http://www.ualberta.ca/ for the University of Alberta in Edmonton

http://www.uregina.ca/ for the University of Regina in Saskatchewan

http://www.utoronto.ca/ for the University of Toronto

http://www.trentu.ca/ for Trent University in Peterborourgh, Ontario

http://www.queensu.ca/ for Queen's University in Kingston, Ontario

http://www.mcgill.ca/ for McGill University in Montreal

http://www.upei.ca/ for the University of Prince Edward Island in Charlottetown

http://www.unb.ca/ for the University of New Brunswick in Fredericton

American college and university home page Internet addresses generally follow this pattern:

http://www.middlebury.edu/ for Middlebury College in Middlebury, Vermont

http://www.harvard.edu/ for Harvard University in Cambridge, Massachusetts

http://www.brynmawr.edu/ for Bryn Mawr College in Bryn Mawr, Pennsylvania

http://www.cornell.edu/ for Cornell University in Ithaca, New York

http://www.umich.edu/ for the University of Michigan in Ann Arbor, Michigan http://www.arizona.edu/ for the University of Arizona in Tucson, Arizona

http://www.reed.edu/ for Reed College in Portland, Oregon

http://www.stanford.edu/ for Stanford University in Stanford, California

http://www.ucdavis.edu/ for the University of California-Davis in Davis, California

If you have trouble finding a school's home page, try searching with one of the Internet search engines. E.g., Yahoo (at http://www.yahoo.com/), Excite, or Alta Vista (at http://www.altavista.digital.com/)

THE PARENT'S GUIDE HOME PAGE

A new home page on the Internet, started by British Columbia parent Peter Cowley, can be reached at http://www.parentsguide.com/. *The Parent's Guide* is still under construction, but it already offers valuable information on secondary and post-secondary schools, scholarships, International Baccalaureate programs, United World Colleges (e.g., Lester B. Pearson College on Vancouver Island), and much more. *The Parent's Guide* also contains a "Forum for Discussion" of education-related topics via e-mail, and an "Ask the Guide" section where individuals can have their questions answered. This innovative Internet site is definitely worth a look.

If you prefer non-computer communication, The *Parent's Guide* can be reached at 3775 W. 12th Ave., Vancouver, B.C. V6R 2N7 or phone/fax (604) 224-8803.

GOING TO UNIVERSITY

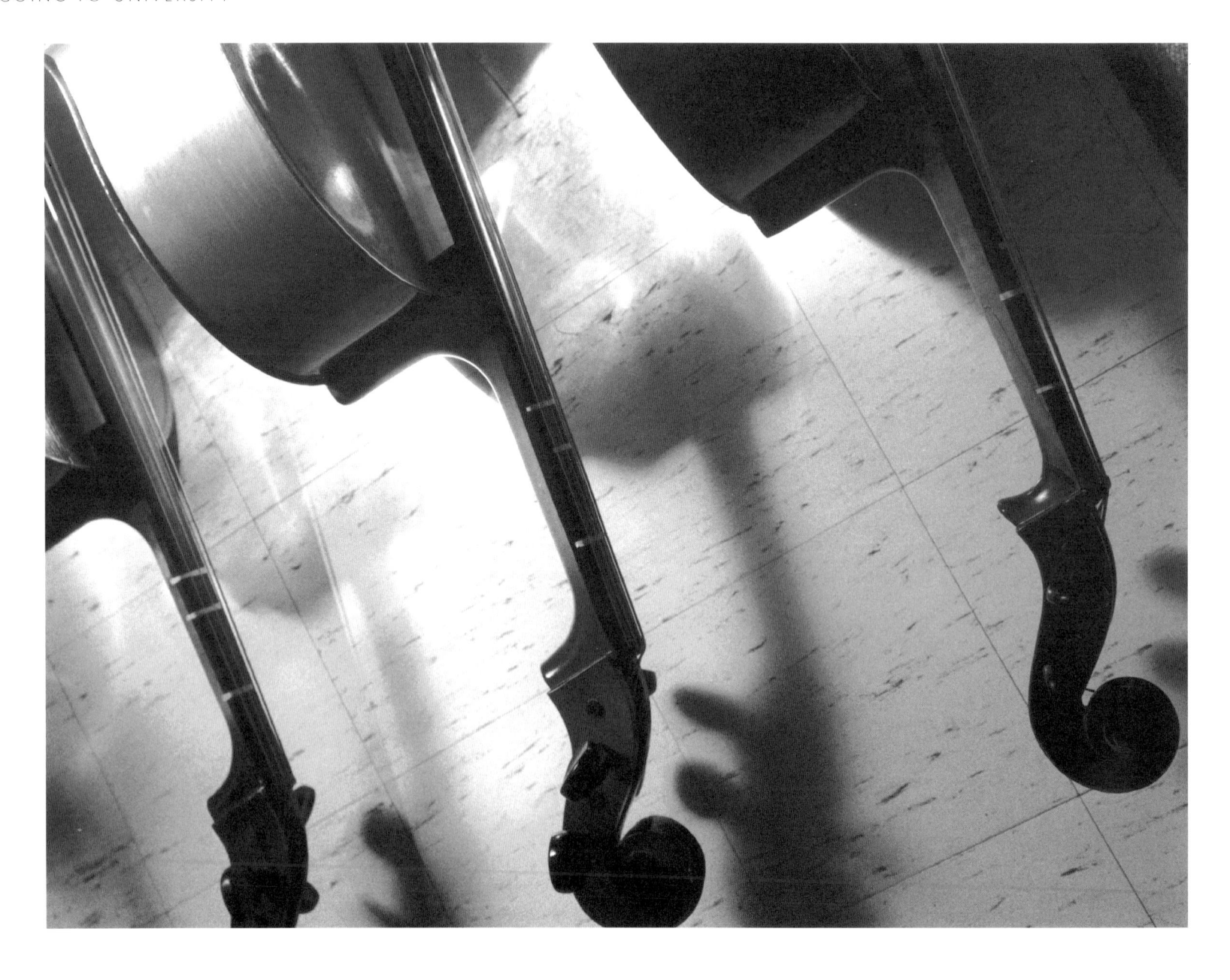

Information on CD-ROMs

The *School Finder* CD-ROM, a new Canadian product, includes information on approximately 220 Canadian colleges and universities and hundreds of scholarships. Facts and figures on enrollment, pictures of the campus, lists of programs, application information, and mission statements are just some of the information schools have chosen to include on *School Finder*. Some Canadian universities have only limited entries on this innovative CD-ROM, but more and more schools are submitting useful information including campus tours with music and student guides. For example, the University of Guelph's entry takes you on a tour of the university highlighting academic opportunities as well as extracurricular activities.

School Finder starts with a number of questions to help match your interests with Canadian universities and colleges. This matching process can prompt you to think about schools you hadn't previously considered, and it can provide information to help you decide which school is the best fit for you and your educational plans.

This CD-ROM is expensive and is intended for high school guidance programs, so ask your guidance counsellor if *School Finder* is available in your high school. (Guidance counsellors can call 1-800-211-5577 to ask about the *School Finder* CD-ROM.)

• An American version of *School Finder*, *Getting Into College*, is produced by *U.S. News and World Report*. Using student "video hosts," icons and buttons, *Getting Into College* starts with a series of questions to help you select colleges and universities that fit your needs and preferences, provides basic information on schools, lists tips on college interviews, makes suggestions for financing your education, gives you tips on planning for dormitory life, and finding study-abroad programs. It also contains articles from *U.S. News and World Report* written in the last ten years, registration information and test dates for standardized tests required by American schools, and much more. The *Getting Into College* CD-ROM is available from Creative Multimedia, 225 SW Broadway, Suite 600, Portland, Oregon U.S.A. 97205, (503) 241-4351 for about $35US.

• The Time-Princeton Review publication, *The Best College for You*, comes with application forms on a CD-ROM. This allows students to apply to a number of American schools electronicallly. (See page 39.)

New CD-ROMS are a good source of information on universities.

INFORMATION ON CD-ROMS

GOING TO UNIVERSITY

Looking for Scholarships and Financial Aid

There is a lot of financial aid available for students, but some of it takes a bit of searching and initiative to find. Taking the time to become informed on scholarships and aid can significantly reduce the expense of a university education, leaving you with less debt upon graduation. Each year many scholarships are not awarded because there have been no suitable applicants, so be sure to apply even if you think your chances are slim.

The terminology involving financial assistance for university students can be confusing. Basic definitions are as follows:

scholarships, bursaries and grants - These are gifts that do not have to be paid back. Scholarships are usually based on academic merit and sometimes on merit, financial need and involvement in specified activities. Bursaries are usually awarded on a combination of academic merit, financial need and involvement in specific activities.

loans - This money has to be paid back, usually after graduation or a set period of time. The interest paid on student loans is usually much less than the normal consumer loan rates offered by financial institutions.

work-study arrangements - These are arrangements where the university provides a student with funds in exchange for the student filling a job, usually on campus. The funds do not have to be repaid because they are payment for work performed.

co-op programs - In co-op programs students alternate between periods of study on campus and paid work, usually off campus. Most co-op programs help students find job placements related to their academic studies. Co-op job wages vary, but these programs allow students to earn money and get valuable work experience while going to school. Co-op programs usually require more time until graduation than regular programs because of the time spent in job placements.

SCHOLARSHIPS FOR CANADIAN UNIVERSITIES

Most Canadian universities offer a wide array of entrance and other scholarships as well as access to financial aid packages available from other sources, usually the government. The amount of money offered by universities varies a great deal, and it can change from year to year. Some schools like the University of Western Ontario, and programs like the University of Alberta's Engineering Faculty, have offered small scholarships to all applicants with high school grade averages above a certain level. Individual colleges within universities (e.g., St. John's College at the University of Manitoba) may also offer scholarships for college members. (See page 78.)

In some cases you must apply for specific scholarships, but in other cases, such as the University of Waterloo's Engineering Faculty, you are automatically considered for scholarships when you are admitted. Some provincial governments, like that of British Columbia, offer scholarships to provincial residents who have top high school grades and then attend a university in that province. To get current information about university-specific scholarships and aid you need to check the literature for each school.

There are also a number of general scholarships not tied to attendance at a specific school (e.g., Terry Fox Scholarship, Canadian Recreational Canoeing Association - Bill Mason Memorial Scholarship). The best way to find out about these general Canadian scholarships, as well as some university specific ones, is by using *Canadian Scholarships on File*, a scholarship CD-ROM that may be available through your school guidance counsellor.

Canadian Scholarships on File comes with a questionnaire designed to match you with potential scholarships. Your answers to questions about your proposed major, province of residence, gender, ethnic background, academic standing and affiliations with various professions and corporations are matched with available scholarship requirements. You then apply individually for scholarships you may have a chance of receiving. *Canadian Scholarships on File* is updated regularly and so is more accurate than published books on scholarships that are usually outdated shortly after they reach the book store. Students should ask their guidance counsellor about using this scholarship data base. (Guidance counsellors can get more information on *Canadian Scholarships on File* by calling 1-800-563-0331, faxing (204) 453-7169 or sending e-mail to

> *Don't overlook the many general scholarships not tied to attendance at a particular school.*

rebecca@cdnscholars.com).

The *Canadian Scholarships on File* data base is also available on the Internet through the *Parent's Guide* site. Parents and students can complete the scholarship questionnaire on-line and get a list of potential scholarships within seconds. The *Parent's Guide* can be reached at http://www.parentsguide.com/.

One book on scholarships that is now dated, but worth a look, is Michael Howell's *Winning Scholarships*. The first section of Howell's book has some very good information on writing for scholarship information and applying for scholarships, but some of the addresses in the book are now inaccurate and a number of the scholarships have been discontinued.

FINANCIAL AID FOR CANADIAN UNIVERSITIES

Canada Student Loans come from the federal government and are interest free while a student is studying full time. Repayment must start six months after a student stops full-time study. Provincial loan programs are also available for residents who are studying full time. In most cases, provincial loan repayment also starts six months after full-time study ends.

Special financial awards or aid may be available from individual provinces for disabled, part-time, and/or Canadian Aboriginal students. Since financial packages and eligibility vary by school and province, detailed information should be requested from the financial aid office of each university you are considering.

SCHOLARSHIPS AND FINANCIAL AID FOR AMERICAN UNIVERSITIES

Many American schools offer only need-based, as opposed to merit-based, scholarships and financial aid. In addition, many forms of aid are only available to United States citizens. One popular guide to financial aid for American schools is the ACT's *Financial Aid Need Estimator*. This is a customized service to help families plan for higher education expenses. It contains scholarship information, cost estimates, grant eligibility and other information on specific schools. To get further information on this service, contact the ACT National Office at P.O. Box 168, Iowa City, Iowa U.S.A. 52243, (319) 337-1000, fax (319) 339-3021.

A second guide to American scholarships is *College Scholarships and Financial Aid* compiled by Wintergreen/Orchard House Inc. This guide profiles over 500,000 publicly available scholarships worth $825million US. The book can be purchased with or without Arco's *Scholarship Search Software*. Arco's interactive software is designed to be user friendly and to make finding potential scholarships fast and easy.

To qualify for a U.S. government federal educational aid package, students and their families must fill out a form called "Free Application for Federal Student Aid." This form is used to calculate the financial contribution to be made by the student and his or her family and eligibility for aid. The submission date for these forms is usually early in January of the student's Grade 12 year. Once the need level is established, a financial aid package from a combination of the government and school can be put together. Aid may be in the form of grants, scholarships, loans, or work-study programs. Most American college guide books (See page 36.) have detailed information on scholarship and financial aid packages available through the government, as well as from individual schools. A table of approximate expected parental contributions toward a student's university education is included in *Peterson's*

Four-Year Colleges. (See page 38.) This table will give you an idea of your eligibility for federal financial aid.

One example of scholarships with a citizenship restriction is the prestigious *Merit Scholarships®*. To be eligible you must: (1) be a United States citizen (or in the process of becoming one), (2) be a full time high school student planning to graduate in the next academic year, (3) take the Preliminary Scholastic Assessment Test/National Merit Scholarship Qualifying Test (PSAT/ NMSQT) no later than Grade 11, and (4) use the scholarship at an American school. The *National Merit Scholarship Program* awards about 6,900 scholarships yearly, and approximately 1,300 additional scholarships are sponsored by corporations and other sponsors through the *Merit Program*. If you qualify for these scholarships ask your guidance counsellor about taking the PSAT/NMSQT (See page 74.), or send a letter to PSAT/NMSQT, P.O. Box 6720, Princeton, New Jersey U.S.A. 08541-6720, call (609) 771-7070, or fax (609) 530-0482 for details.

Some schools offer scholarships on the basis of merit without considering either citizenship or need. Since these scholarships are usually unique to each school, it is necessary to contact the schools you are interested in to ask about this type of financial aid.

ATHLETIC SCHOLARSHIPS IN PARTICULAR

One service that looks for scholarships for student athletes is *College Prospects of America* (CPOA). For a service fee, CPOA will compile a profile for a student and help match him or her with schools in the United States and Canada which offer opportunities and scholarships for student athletes. CPOA works through regional representatives, and prepares materials which are sent to prospective colleges and universities. Ask your guidance counsellor for information on CPOA and

Some U.S. schools offer scholarships on the basis of merit where citizenship and need are not taken into account.

other athletic scholarship services. The central Canadian CPOA representative can be reached at (204) 256-5008 or 1-800-665-5604. The CPOA head office can be reached at 1-800-432-2762 or on the Internet at http://www. CPOA.com/.

Get Yourself a College Sports Scholarship by Susan M. Wilson is also a valuable source of information on how to be recruited for college teams and sports scholarships. This book, by a top coach, provides information on American athletic scholarships.

GOING TO UNIVERSITY

Visiting Universities

A campus visit is probably the best way to get to know a school. Although a visit to an out-of-province school can be expensive, you may consider it worth the cost to get a first hand feel for the place where you may spend the next three or four years, as well as thousands of dollars. Many students 'know' a school is 'right' for them after a campus visit.

One Day Two Schools, Two Days Three Schools

You can visit a school anytime, but you'll get the best feel for campus life if you visit while regular classes are in session. This means going during your high school year, but with some planning you can arrange a trip on one of your teachers' in-service days, during spring break, or some other time when you'll miss as few days of school as possible.

You may be able to visit two schools in one day. For example, Université d' Ottawa in the morning and Carleton University in the afternoon, Simon Fraser University in the morning and the University of British Columbia in the afternoon, York University in the morning and the University of Toronto in the afternoon, Waterloo University in the morning and Wilfrid Laurier University in the afternoon, the University of Manitoba in the morning and the University of Winnipeg in the afternoon. It's also possible to do an intensive two day trip and visit several schools. For instance, the University of Victoria one day and the University of British Columbia and Simon Fraser the next, the University of Western Ontario one day and the Universities of Guelph and Waterloo the next day, Queen's University one day and McGill University and Université de Montréal the next day, Dalhousie University one day and Mount Saint Vincent and Saint Mary's University the next day, the University of Regina one day and the University of Saskatchewan the next, the University of Alberta one day and the University of Calgary the next, and Mount Allison University one day and St. Thomas University and the University of New Brunswick the next day. Many other combinations can be arranged if you have one or more days.

The Tour

Most schools are set up for visitors during the fall term. Once you pick your dates, call the university secondary school liaison or admission office and sign up for a tour. Daily student-led tours are usually offered at set times. Most tours provide you with an overview of the campus, a visit to a residence, the library, bookstore, computer and sports facilities, and maybe they'll even point out favorite campus hang-outs. A tour is also a good time to ask questions of your student guide, and to hear answers to questions asked by other students and parents on the tour.

If you are interested in becoming a member of a college that is part of the university you're visiting, be sure to make it a part of your visit. Even a quick visit can give you an idea of the opportunities and atmosphere at the college. (See page 78.)

Following the formal tour, you can request that arrangements be made for you to sit in on classes, talk to advisors, students, and/or professors in programs of particular interest to you. If you want to sit in on a class, the school will usually give you a list of several classes that are open to visitors. You may want to talk to an athletic coach, see the athletic facilities, and sit in on a team practice, or you may want to look through the library and check specific collections. Maybe you'll prefer to wander around campus, read bulletin boards, talk to students you meet, and have something to eat in the student union or campus hang-out. If you call several weeks ahead, arrangements can be made for you to talk to and see just about anybody and anything of interest to you.

HOW TO INTERVIEW A SCHOOL

Ideally you want to interview a university during a campus visit by talking to an admissions counsellor, professors from specific departments, and/or students. This lets you form your own impressions of the school and get all your questions answered. However, if a physical tour isn't possible, a phone or e-mail conversation with an admissions officer, followed by a rereading of the school's printed or electronic information, is the next best alternative.

There are many questions that you can ask when you interview a university. These suggestions can help you make your own list of 10 to 20 questions to ask an admissions officer when you visit or call a school.

SOME QUESTIONS TO ASK

Classes and Advising

How big are average first year classes?

Are first year classes taught by experienced professors or by graduate students?

Do large lecture classes usually have smaller discussion classes?

Are classes small enough in first and/or second year that professors can learn most student's names?

What is the school's student to professor ratio?

Can third and fourth year undergraduate students work one-on-one with a professor on research projects?

Who will be my advisor?

How many other students will be assigned to my advisor?

Are students treated like numbers or individuals? Ask for examples of students being treated as individuals if this is important to you.

Computers, Laboratories, and the Libraries

How many computer labs are on campus and what are their opening hours?

Do computer labs have enough machines to accommodate student demand during busy periods?

Will I be expected to purchase my own computer? If so, what kind do you advise?

Does the university offer educational discount prices for students who purchase computers? If so, where could you get a list of current prices?

What computer support services are available to students and what are their hours? Is there support for both PC and MAC users?

Are individual residence rooms hard-wired for computers to provide easy access to the Internet and e-mail?

Are students given their own e-mail account free of charge?

How large are laboratory classes?

What kind of scientific equipment does the school own? How up-to-date is the equipment?

How many libraries are on campus? Are all of them open to undergraduates?

Have library acquisitions kept up with the growing printed and electronic knowledge base?

Curriculum and Student Life

Does the school have courses, programs, and/or majors in areas of interest to you?

How long will it take to register for courses, and how is this done?

Do certain students have preferential treatment in registration? If so, who are they?

Do first year students tend to get their first choice of courses, time slots, and professors?

What student support services are available - tutors, writing assistance, learning skills programs, counseling? Are these services offered free of charge? If not, what are the charges?

Students can learn a lot from their classmates. Do students get together outside of class? How does this happen?

Does the school support activities that help students to get to know each other? If so, what are some of these?

Is there an orientation program for first year students? If so, get some details on the timing and activities.

Does the school offer an 'Introduction to University' course or a 'transition year' program to help first year students make the shift from high school to university?

What food service is available on campus? What are the best places to eat on campus? Can students with special diets be readily accommodated by campus food service?

Are there many restaurants close to campus? Do students receive discounts at these restaurants?

What percentage of students live in residence? What percentage live within a half a mile of campus?

If it's a commuter school, what time do most students arrive on campus and when do most leave? (You can often tell this by observing activity in the student parking lots.) Do students tend to schedule their classes on Tuesday/Thursday or Monday/Wednesday/Friday and not come to campus the days they don't have classes?

What happens in the evenings? Are there many students around, in the library, at student club activities, participating in intramural sports? Do students come in for evening classes and then leave?

What happens on weekends? Are there many students around, in the library, at student club activities, participating in intramural sports? Are students who come on the weekend just there for class and then they leave?

For residential campuses, ask if it's a 'suitcase' school where many students go home or leave for the weekend.

Do students attend school athletic events? If so, which ones? Is there much school spirit?

Are arts and cultural events plentiful on campus? If so, what are they and what are the costs? If not, where can students go for arts and cultural events?

Are university drama, musical or other arts productions open to student participants who aren't majoring in these disciplines?

What opportunities exist for students to develop or practice multi-lingual abilities on campus?

Are there colleges associated with the university that students can join or live in? If so, how is each college unique and what special opportunities does it offer? What are the membership requirements for each college?

Financial Questions

How many entrance scholarships are available that you could be eligible to receive? Do entrance scholarships continue on to second year and beyond? If so, are there requirements you must meet to continue to receive scholarship monies?

Are entrance scholarships automatically given to students entering with high school grade averages above a certain level? If so, what is that average?

What scholarships are available for students beyond first year?

What student loans are available? How would you apply for them? What pay-back requirements are attached to these?

Are student jobs available on campus? If so, what is the general wage range? How hard is it to get these jobs?

Are there summer job placement services available?

Graduation

What is the drop-out rate for students during and after first year? You may want to ask this question for the university as a whole and for particular faculties, schools and/or departments.

How long does it take most students to graduate with a bachelor's degree? Three years? Four years? Five years?

What percentage of students enroll in 3-year, 4-year, and Honours programs in disciplines or professions of interest to you?

What percent of graduates in disciplines or professions of interest to you get jobs in their fields directly after graduation? How many go on to professional or graduate school to earn advanced degrees?

What career and/or graduate counseling services does the school provide? Is there a fee for this service?

What have alumni done with degrees in disciplines of interest to you?

Is there an active alumni association? Do alumni provide generous financial support to the school?

Other

Can you receive university credit for Advanced Placement (AP) courses you have taken in high school?

Are there special organizations or support programs for Aboriginal, adult, single-parent and/or disabled students?

Is there provision for academic exchanges with other Canadian or American schools? If so, which schools, and what are the exchanges like?

Is there provision for study abroad? If so, what countries are involved, and how many students take advantage of the programs?

GOING TO UNIVERSITY

Applications and Admission Requirements

Admission requirements vary greatly by school. Some schools pride themselves on being highly selective; others are equally proud that their open admission policies make them accessible to most interested students. The majority of Canadian schools have admissions standards that place them somewhere between these two extremes.

All admissions policies have strengths and weaknesses, so it is important to consider the implications of these policies when selecting a university. When a school is highly selective in its admissions criteria, the academic abilities of its students will be very similar, and professors will assume a well-prepared student body. The intellectual atmosphere may be exciting and stimulating, and the environment may be competitive. The campus culture at some highly selective schools is one where everyone works hard and plays hard. On the other hand, when a school has an open admission policy that admits students with a range of high school averages from the low 60's to the high 90's, the student body will be diverse in its abilities, and professors will adapt their teaching and expectations to that diversity. Exceptional students may have to look harder to find an intellectually stimulating and exciting group of peers at an open admission school, and the academic atmosphere may be more laid back than competitive. Admissions standards can also vary between programs within a school, so ask the school or your guidance counsellor for the entering high school grade ranges and averages for the universities and programs that you are considering.

CANADIAN UNIVERSITIES

The Application Process

Canadian universities place a great deal of emphasis on Grade 11 and 12 grades and completion of certain high school mathematics, social science, English and science courses when deciding on admission. Many schools also ask for information on high school awards and scholarships, leadership positions held, extracurricular activities, and special circumstances that may have influenced high school performance. Some schools will give you credit for Advanced Placement (AP) courses from high school, but others will not. Some may consider the university performance of previous graduates from your high school, but many others do not. As competition to attend some universities increases, they may start to ask for more information and take it into account in their admission decisions. Asking

APPLICATIONS AND ADMISSION REQUIREMENTS

for more information will allow schools to select the students that they think will do best in and benefit the most from popular programs.

If you think that completing a school's application form does not provide an accurate reflection of your activities and achievements, you may want to include a résumé with your application. Résumés are not required, but if your experiences and circumstances are out of the ordinary, a résumé will give the admissions office better information on which to base its decision. Bookstores and libraries usually carry several books to help you write a résumé. One that is especially useful for students is *Your First Resume* by Ron Fry.

Letters of reference and admission essays are generally not part of the application requirements for Canadian universities, but this may change in the future. Standardized test scores, such as the SAT and ACT (See page 73.), are also not required for Canadian university admission, but students who have written these tests are free to send their scores to schools.

Application deadlines are usually in the spring or summer of the student's Grade 12 year. Universities send acceptance notices from February to mid- or late summer. Some schools will accept students on the basis of their Grade 12 mid-year grades on the condition that their marks don't fall before graduation. Other schools want to see final Grade 12 marks before they accept students.

Scholarship notification dates also vary widely. Some schools make scholarship offers in the spring and others wait until mid- or late summer before making their offers.

Application deadlines and requirements vary by university and province, so you should check with your high school guidance counsellor for detailed information. If your counsellor does not have the forms and information that you need, you can check a university's home page on the Internet for application information.

Admissions standards vary widely between schools, and may even vary between programs at the same school.

More and more universities are allowing students to apply electronically via the Internet, sending official high school transcripts and other material later by traditional mail.

Admission Standards

Admission requirements vary widely. However, even when a university tells you that a certain high school average is the minimum cutoff for admission, it doesn't mean you'll be admitted with that average. Many programs have limited enrollments and students with the highest grade point averages are taken first. This may mean that no applicants near the minimum cutoff are accepted.

If you're looking for a quick comparison of average entering grades at various universities, the annual *Maclean's* rankings issue (See page 33.) is an easy place to find the information. When you look at these numbers remember that they are averages. The distribution around the average may be quite small (i.e., most entering students had high school averages very close to the *Maclean's* reported average) or quite wide (i.e., many entering students had high school averages well below or above the *Maclean's* reported average). Another thing to remember with the *Maclean's* figures is that they are averages based on the entire first year entering class, but the entering average for various programs within that university may vary widely because of the popularity or restrictiveness of particular programs. For example, the 1995 *Maclean's* ranking for Waterloo University reports an average entering high school grade average of 83.9% while the actual high school grades for those enrolled in the popular computer engineering co-op program ranged from the high 80's to the low 90's.

AMERICAN COLLEGES AND UNIVERSITIES

American schools usually require more application information from students than do Canadian schools. While the requirements vary, the minimum application requirements for most American schools are completion of certain high school mathematics, social science, English and science courses, a transcript showing courses and grades from Grades 9 to 12, SAT I, SAT II and/or ACT scores (See page 74.), and the school's admission form. Many of the more selective schools require letters of reference from one or more high school teachers, an employer, a peer, an essay on a topic selected by the school, and sometimes an evaluative oral interview. Application deadlines for schools can be as early as December or as late as March or April.

Public or state-supported American schools usually charge different fees for state residents than for out-of-state students. The out-of-state fees are much higher and can approach the fees charged by private schools. As a result, you may want to check with schools to see if you're eligible for scholarships and/or financial aid. (See page 56.) Examples of U.S. public schools include the University of Michigan, University of California-Berkeley, Ohio State University, Auburn University, and Rutgers University. Examples of private schools include Georgetown University, Harvard University, Northwestern University, University of Notre Dame, and Massachusetts Institute of Technology.

Some American schools offer early admission decisions for students who apply in the fall of their Grade 12 year. Students who apply under the early decision application process are usually asked to promise that they will attend if they are admitted. Some schools have a "rolling admissions policy" which means that they accept qualified students when they apply until all the spaces are filled.

An increasing number of American schools allow you to apply for admission through their Internet sites. Application software, such as *Apply*, gives you electronic access to more than one hundred application forms. If you're interested in the software, send e-mail to apply@aol.com or write to *Apply Software*, 30 East 90th Street, New York, New York U.S.A. 10128. *Apply* software also comes with the 1996 issue of the Time-Princeton Review's *The Best College for You*.

Two guides designed to help students and their parents with the admissions and application process for American colleges and universities are:

1) College Admissions: A Crash Course for Panicked Parents by Sally Rubenstone and Sidonia Dalby is a practical guide that offers valuable advice for parents. It explains what parents and students can expect at every stage of the admissions process, provides advice on encouraging a student through the process, and gives valuable information on helping students make the best choice of schools.

2) College Applications and Essays: A How-to Handbook by Susan D. Van Raalte takes students through ten simple steps to help them produce an outstanding college or university application and write an exceptional admissions essay. The guide has useful worksheets, checklists and examples which make it easy for both students and parents to use.

STANDARDIZED TESTS USED FOR ADMISSIONS

Almost all American colleges and universities require students to take standardized tests that measure knowledge as well as problem-solving and analytical abilities. Canadian universities do not require these tests, but students may elect to send their scores to provide admissions officers with additional information.

Because competition can be rigorous for admission to selective American schools, and because standardized test scores (e.g., SAT and ACT) are so important in the selection process, many students prepare for these tests by taking special preparatory courses (e.g., The Princeton Review and Kaplan Educational Centers offer popular preparation courses), working with special guides or studying old exams. One of these guides is The Princeton Review's *Cracking the SAT & PSAT,* by Adam Robinson and John Katzman. *Cracking the SAT & PSAT* injects a great deal of humour into an otherwise dry and serious topic. The authors introduce you to the SAT test

APPLICATIONS AND ADMISSION REQUIREMENTS

writers, build your confidence, discuss test-taking skills, provide a guide to pacing yourself during the test, and include several hundred questions and answers from past tests. Other test preparation manuals are available at most bookstores.

The following are the required and optional standardized tests for admission to most American colleges and universities:

ACT (American College Test) - The ACT is designed to assess a student's general educational development and ability to be successful in university for the areas covered by the test. The ACT reports twelve scores. Of these, four are test scores in English, mathematics, reading and science reasoning, a composite score, and sub scores in specific areas on the English, math and reading tests. American colleges and universities may require the ACT for admission consideration or they may accept ACT scores in place of SAT I and SAT II scores. The ACT is administered five times a year in the U. S. and four times a year in Canada. Ask your guidance counsellor for testing dates and locations, or write

American College Testing, P.O. Box 168, Iowa City, Iowa, U.S.A. 52243. (319) 337-1000, fax (319) 399-3021.

PSAT (Preliminary Scholastic Assessment Test) - The PSAT provides practice for Grade 10 and 11 students who plan to take the SAT I in the spring of their Grade 11 year or the fall of Grade 12. The PSAT is divided into four sections of 30 minutes each, two testing verbal skills and two testing mathematical reasoning. The PSAT is often described as the PSAT/NMSQT (National Merit Scholarship Qualifying Test) because test results are used to determine eligibility for National Merit Scholarships. (See page 57.) Students should talk to their high school guidance counsellor if they are interested in taking the PSAT.

SAT I (Scholastic Assessment Test) - The SAT I is a three-hour test, with mostly multiple choice questions, that measures verbal and mathematical reasoning abilities.

Many students prepare for the ACT and SAT with special courses and guides.

Tests dates are usually in November, December, January, May and June with registration deadlines about six weeks earlier. American schools may require applicants to take the SAT rather than the ACT. Numerous testing sites are available in Canada and the U.S. Registration forms are available through high school guidance counsellors or by writing College Board SAT Program, P.O. Box 6200, Princeton, New Jersey, U.S.A. 08541-6200. Toll free registration from Canada is available by calling 1-800-728-7267.

SAT II (Scholastic Assessment Test: Subject Tests, formerly called Achievement Tests) - The SAT II is a series of one hour tests, with mostly multiple choice questions, in 14 specific subject areas that test subject-specific knowledge and the ability to apply it. One or more of these subject tests may be required by American schools for admission or placement. Numerous testing dates and sites are available in Canada and the U.S. Registration forms are available through high school guidance counsellors or by writing College Board SAT Program, P.O. Box 6200, Princeton, New Jersey, U.S.A. 08541-6200. Toll free registration from Canada is available by calling 1-800-728-7267.

Students receive their scores, about seven weeks after they write these standardized tests, and so do the colleges and universities to whom the student requested the scores be sent. These standardized tests are taken by many thousands of students around the world which allows individuals to compare their results against a large group of peers. Score reports tell students their individual scores as well as their percentile rankings. For instance, students who score in the 90th percentile know that they performed better on the test than 90 percent of the others who wrote it. American college guides (See page 37.) usually report the average or range of SAT and ACT scores for the first year (freshman) class at each college and university.

Students receive their standardized test scores about seven weeks after writing the test.

High school guidance counsellors and book stores usually have numerous guides for students planning to take these standardized tests. Guidance counsellors may also be able to tell students about special PSAT/SAT and ACT preparatory courses offered in their area.

GOING TO UNIVERSITY

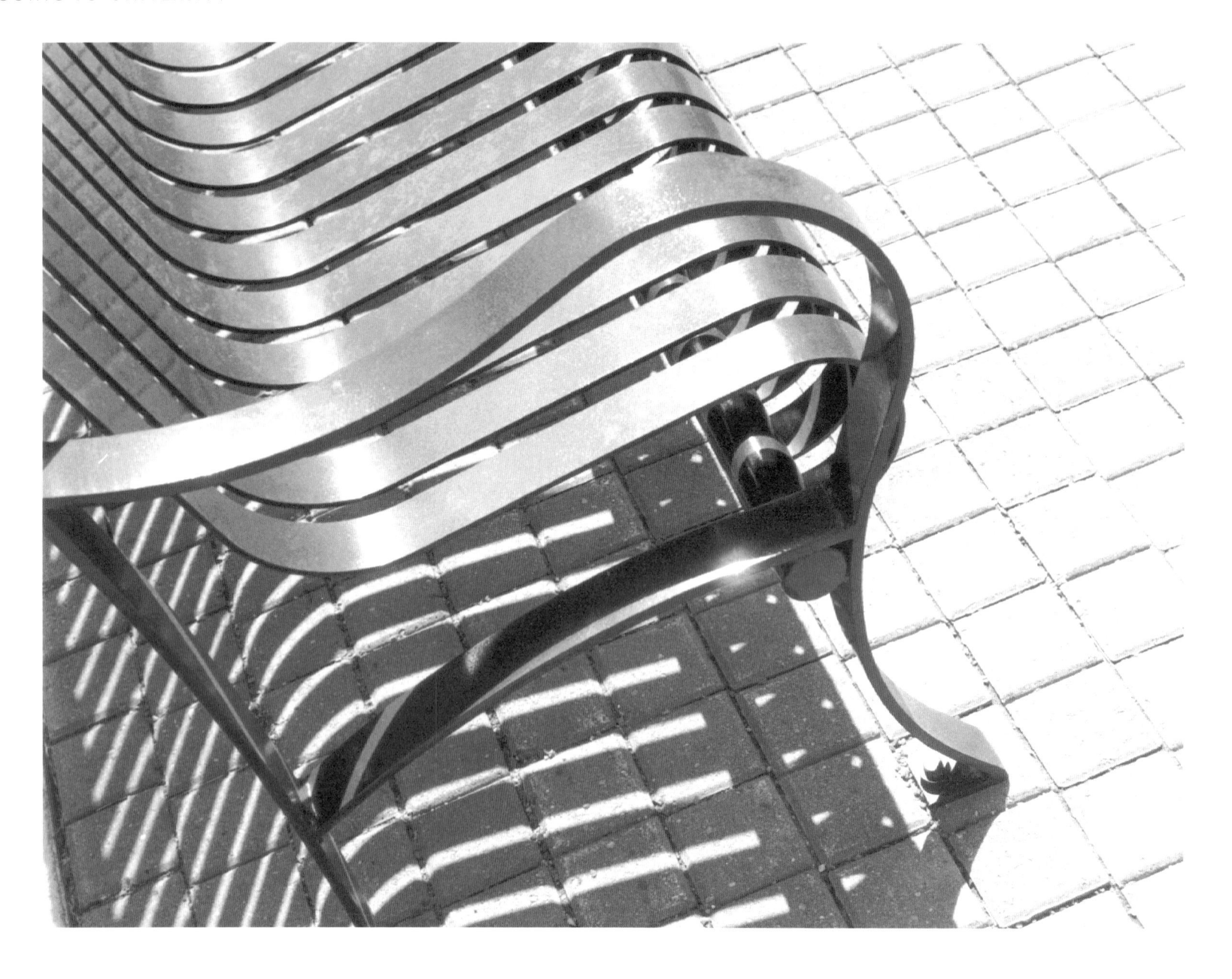

Small Colleges within Large Universities

Many large Canadian universities have small member colleges located on their campuses. These small colleges, some of which come with their own residence and food service, can provide the opportunity for small classes, a group of like-minded students, social activities, scholarships, the friendliness of a small group, and special courses for college members. Some colleges have affiliations with religious organizations, but may not require that college members practice that religion or even attend the college's religious activities.

> **Students who think they might find a large university overwhelming should investigate the possibility of joining a college.**

Some colleges are the central focus of a student's university experience. Others are little more than a residence with some social activities. However, students who think they might find a large university overwhelming should investigate the possibility of joining a college.

King's College on the Dalhousie University campus is one such college. King's has about 700 students, a strong sense of community, a popular Foundation Year Program where students study Western civilization's great books, and a friendly rivalry with Dalhousie. Students take many classes with Dal students and degrees from King's are co-signed by Dalhousie.

Huron, King's and Brescia Colleges on the University of Western Ontario campus are other examples of popular small colleges within a larger university. Each of these colleges has a residence, its own classes, and a sense of camaraderie. Students at all three colleges take some classes on the Western campus. Brescia is an all-female college run by Roman Catholic nuns, Huron has Anglican affiliations and King's was originally a Catholic college for men, but is now co-ed. Each college has its own special culture and traditions.

Many other colleges exist within large universities. Examples include the University of Manitoba's connections with University College, St. John's, St. Paul's and St. Andrew's Colleges on its main campus as well as ties with the Collège universitaire de Saint Boniface. The University of Regina is affiliated with Campion College, Saskatchewan Indian Federated College, and Luther College. The University of Saskatchewan is associated with St. Thomas More College. The University of Toronto's main campus has ties to University, Trinity, Victoria, New, Woodsworth, Innis, and St. Michael's Colleges. The University of Waterloo is affiliated with St. Jerome's,

Conrad Grebel, St. Paul's and Renison Colleges. Other Canadian universities also have associations with small colleges.

Each of these colleges offer choices within a large university. Choices that may provide the right fit between a student and a school.

GOING TO UNIVERSITY

Distance Education

Many Canadian universities offer courses by distance education that may be ideal for students who cannot attend classes on campus or at a specific time. Some distance courses involve a text, a set of assignments you complete at home, the final exam, and occasional phone contact with the instructor. Others involve lecture classes accessed by TV from your home, students meeting in a variety of locations to participate in a live-video link with the instructor and students at other locations, and courses via the Internet. As technology develops, the possibilities for delivery of distance education also increase. These changes allow distant students to have many of the advantages of an on-campus classroom without the inconvenience or time commitment of travel.

You'll find that many universities offer distance education programs but that they may specialize in certain kinds of delivery. E.g., regional program delivery, the far north, correspondence-type courses, Master's of Business Administration (MBA) programs. At some universities it is possible to complete all the requirements for a degree through distance education, while other schools only offer a few courses in each discipline.

Two universities that specialize in distance education are Athabasca University in Athabasca, Alberta (P.O. Box 10000, T0G 2R0, (403) 675-6168, e-mail auinfo@admin.athabascau.ca) and the British Columbia Open University in Burnaby, B.C. (c/o Open Learning Agency, 4355 Mathissi Place, Burnaby, B.C. V5G 4S8, (604) 431-3000, e-mail studentserv@ola.bc.ca). Athabasca offers degree programs in computer science and a variety of liberal arts disciplines, and certificate programs in many other areas. The Open University offers degree programs in several arts and science disciplines, but courses with laboratory or workshop requirements are open only to British Columbia residents.

Two of many other schools with established distance education programs are the University of Manitoba which has courses for students in Manitoba and all over the world, and the University of Waterloo which offers numerous courses, some via the Internet. As learning technologies expand, many schools are adding to their distance delivery offerings or are starting distance programs, so you should contact a number of schools if you'd like to enroll in a distance education program.

> *Distance education courses may be ideal for students who cannot attend classes on campus.*

DISTANCE EDUCATION

GOING TO UNIVERSITY

Leaving Home for University

Going to university involves changes if you stay at home or if you go away. Even if you stay home, you'll have much more independence than in high school. You'll have to organize your time and studying on your own, you may be in very large classes, and some of the subjects you study may be new to you. In addition, you'll have to find the buildings where your classes are located and learn your way around campus, become familiar with the university rules and regulations, and be among people you've never met before. At first, you may wonder if you're up to the academic challenges, and you may generally feel a bit overwhelmed. If you add moving away from home, living on your own, meeting hundreds of new people, and making new friends to the list of changes, going to university is even more challenging. You'll definitely be adding some stress to your life, but if you have ensured a good fit between yourself and the school, it will also be an exciting and intellectually stimulating experience.

Having some days where you're feeling a bit homesick, wondering if all this was a good idea, missing your high school friends and maybe a boy or girlfriend, missing family members and your dog/cat/horse are to be expected. If you're at a selective school, you will probably find that your first university marks aren't nearly as high as those you earned in high school, and this may make you wonder if you can do well academically. Most first year students have all of these feelings at one time or another.

Having some days where you're feeling a bit stressed is to be expected.

Dealing With the Transition

How do you deal with all of this change? Here are some suggestions:

1) Make sure you attend all parts of any orientation program your university has for first year students. These sessions immerse you in the campus culture and traditions, give you valuable information about the school's rules and regulations, introduce you to advisors, administrators and older students who can answer your questions, familiarize you with the campus, and allow you to meet other students who are having the same thoughts and feelings you're having. Staying in your room for the first few weeks isn't a good idea because you'll miss getting yourself off on the right foot.

2) Join a student organization or club, become active in your residence organization, and/or join an intramural sports team. This will introduce you to new people, help you make friends, and get you involved with life on campus. Becoming involved and active will make the transition to university a lot easier.

3) Seek out older students from your high school who have already been at your university a year or two. Ask them how they dealt with the concerns that you're facing.

4) Call home and talk to your family. Some moral support or a care package from home can be very reassuring and a real tonic, even if the first few calls or packages leave you a bit homesick.

5) Call high school friends at other universities to commiserate and share solutions to problems with being in university.

6) Talk to your professor if you're having concerns about a particular course, assignment or test. Professors have office hours where they're available to talk to students. Don't hesitate to ask for help or advice. This is part of what they are paid for.

7) Talk to your residence floor advisor or a counsellor at your university's student services centre. They'll listen and help you solve specific problems. It's their job to be there for students.

8) Go to the student study skills office if you have concerns about writing essays, taking multiple choice exams, test anxiety, reading too slowly, organizing your time, or any other academic question. These offices usually have counsellors who can talk to you one-on-one and and they may offer short workshops to improve your study skills. It's the job of these offices to help students develop academic skills.

9) Remember that universities, especially highly selective schools, screen all their applicants to pick those most likely to succeed. They picked you because they thought that you had the academic talent, maturity, and general ability to succeed at university. The university that you're attending wants you to succeed as much as you do, and they have all sorts of resources in place to help make your university experience a good one.

10) At least some of the time, relax and enjoy yourself! Going to university, can be a great deal of fun. Don't study all the time.

THINGS TO TAKE IF YOU'RE LEAVING HOME FOR UNIVERSITY

These suggestions were generously provided by Linda Radcliffe whose two sons spent their first university year in residence.

You'll obviously want to take your clothes, toiletry items, personal medications, a calculator, pens and pencils, but there are a few other things you may want to consider that could make life a bit more comfortable.

- small table fan; the fall and spring can be warm if your room isn't air conditioned
- hangers; residence rooms rarely come with hangers
- small refrigerator; small (e.g., 5 cu. feet) refrigerators are available for rent on most campuses for about $100 for the school year
- extra long phone cord; in case your room's jack isn't in a convenient place
- duplex plug for the telephone jack; if your computer modem doesn't support an auxiliary phone
- phone answering machine; you may be able to rent an 'invisible' answering service from the phone company or you may prefer to bring your own machine
- check on long distance telephone calling plans to make phoning home as inexpensive as possible
- floor or table lamp
- small bulletin board and push pins; some residence rooms have bulletin boards, but they never have push pins
- unbreakable plate, bowl, cup, glass, knife, fork, spoon, paring knife, microwave bowls, stirring spoon, medium-size cooking pan, frying pan, dishcloth, and a dishtowel; for late night snacks or when you miss mealtimes
- box of plastic bags
- case of juice boxes
- can opener
- a few cans/boxes of easily made food
- popcorn or other snacks
- alarm clock
- CDs or tapes

- stereo
- personal stereo and earphones
- first aid kit
- cold/hot gel pack
- Swiss Army knife
- screwdriver, pliers, and small hammer
- bedding if the residence doesn't supply it; pillow, pillow case, sheets, quilt or blankets
- bath towels, hand towels and wash cloths
- bathroom caddy; to take your soap, shampoo, razor, toothpaste, etc. to the bathroom
- small bedside rug
- roll of quarters or loonies for the washing/pop machine
- laundry bag
- laundry detergent and supplies
- computer; remember that many schools offer educational discounts on computer purchases by registered students, so you may want to buy one when you get to school
- computer supplies
- surge protector for your computer
- security lock for your computer if you're concerned about theft
- warranty information for the computer
- posters and pictures for your room and something to hang or stick them up with; many residences charge for damage to walls and paint, so ask what they want you to hang things with
- rain gear
- hair dryer

Documents to take with you

- provincial health insurance card
- out-of-province health insurance coverage card if you're leaving your home province; many provinces won't cover you fully while you're out of province unless you let them know you're attending school and will return at the end of the academic year
- Social Insurance Number
- credit card, with a separate record of the number, expiry date, and where to call if the card is lost or stolen

Many schools offer educational discounts on computer purchases by registered students, so you may want to wait until you get to school to buy a computer.

GOING TO UNIVERSITY

If you're leaving your home province to go to school check on an out-of-province health insurance card.

- bank account numbers
- bank book and bank convenience card
- immunization record
- driver's license
- automobile registration and insurance forms, if you're taking a car

LEAVING HOME FOR UNIVERSITY

GOING TO UNIVERSITY

Other Educational Possibilities

SUMMER OPPORTUNITIES FOR GRADE 10 TO 12 STUDENTS

If you prefer to travel or try something new and academically challenging during your high school summers, there are a large number of opportunities available. The programs listed below are but a few of the many that exist. Most interesting summer programs require a financial outlay for participants, but many programs offer scholarships and financial aid to qualified participants.

AFS Interculture Canada, 1231 St. Catherine Street West, Suite 505, Montreal, Quebec H3G 1P5. (514) 288-3282, 1-800-361-7248 (Eastern Canada), 1-800-361-1879 (Western Canada and Newfoundland) - AFS organizes international exchange programs which give students the opportunity to live with host families in another country for the summer. Exchanges are arranged in more than 20 countries around the world.

Carleton College Summer Writing Program, Office of Summer Academic Programs, Northfield, Minnesota U.S.A. 55057. 1-507-663-4038, Internet http://www.carleton.edu/ - This intensive three-week July writing program is for students who have completed Grades 11 or 12. It attracts students from all over the United States and the world. Carleton College is a top-rated liberal arts college in a small town just south of Minneapolis. Weekend trips to Minneapolis/St. Paul are included. The program is designed to help students polish all kinds of writing skills, and is in no way remedial in nature. Basic word processing skills are also taught to students who request them.

Deep River Science Academy, Att: Kathy Hughes, National Registrar, Box 600, Deep River, Ontario K0J 1P0. (613) 584-4541, 1-800-760-DRSA, fax (613) 584-9597, Internet http://intranet.ca/~drsa/, e-mail DRSA@intranet.ca - DRSA offers six week summer opportuinities for students to work on real science or engineering research projects. Programs are offered in: (1) Deep River, ON, 200 km northwest of Ottawa, (2) near Pinawa, MB, 100 km northeast of Winnipeg, and (3) in Kelowna, BC. The programs are designed for students who are thinking of a career in science or engineering, have good grades, approach scientific subjects with enthusiasm and curiosity, and who enjoy working with others of their age. Students must be between the ages of 15 and 19 to participate. All-inclusive costs for the six weeks are $3,700; generous bursaries are available for students who qualify for financial assistance.

OTHER EDUCATIONAL POSSIBILITIES

EF International Language Schools, 60 Bloor Street West, Suite 405, Toronto, Ontario M4W 3B8. (416) 323-0330, 1-800-387-1463, fax (416) 927-8664 - Languages courses in additive two-week modules are offered in Spain, Italy, France and Germany with options for differing levels of instruction intensity. Students have several options for cultural experiences in their free-time.

Harvard University Summer School, Secondary School Program, 51 Brattle Street, Cambridge, Massachusetts U.S.A. 02138-3722. (617) 495-3192 - Harvard's program, for students who have completed Grades 11 or 12, offers a wide variety of academically challenging courses in Anthropology, Biochemistry, Celtic Languages and Literatures, Computer Science, Dramatic Arts, Economics, Japanese, Quantitative Reasoning, Mathematics, Visual and Environmental Sciences and many more disciplines. Participants have the opportunity to participate in the Summer School Chorus, Orchestra, or Pops Band. Students live in residences, and use the many resources of Harvard University. A College Choices Program helps students make decisions about their academic future, offers trips to New England colleges, and hosts a large college fair.

Operation Catapult, Rose-Hulman Institute of Technology, 5500 Wabash Avenue, Terre Haute, Indiana U.S.A. 47803-9959. (812) 877-1511, #8210 for Admissions, Internet http://www.rose-hulman.edu/ - This three-week problem-solving program is for students who have: (1) just completed Grade 11, (2) done well on the PSAT exam, (3) completed three years of high school math, and one year of chemistry or physics, and (4) an interest in an engineering, physics, chemistry or mathematics career. Operation Catapult allows students to work on real-life problems using Rose-Hulman's modern laboratory equipment. Rose-Hulman is a small, top-ranked, co-ed, undergraduate school that is noted for its applied engineering programs and excellence in teaching.

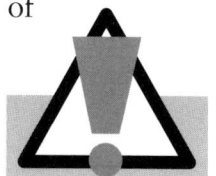

There are many academically challenging summer programs available for high school students.

Sea Education Association, P.O. Box 6, Woods Hole, Massachusetts U.S.A. 02543. (508) 540-3954, fax (508) 457-4673 - For those interested in oceanography, marine ecosystems, ocean navigation, and ocean pollution, this program offers four weeks of lectures, seminars, field trips, labs, and workshops followed by four weeks at sea. While at sea you are an integral part of the crew and research team. This 8-week summer session is associated with SEA Semester (12 weeks). Most participants are university students, but some Grade 12 graduates participate in the program.

Shad Valley Summer Program, c/o Canadian Centre for Creative Technology, 8 Young Street East, Waterloo, Ontario N2J 2L3. (519) 884-8844, fax (519) 884-8191, Internet http://www.shads.org/ - The Shad Valley Summer Program is a four-week opportunity for selected Grade 11 and 12 students to come together on Canadian university campuses to explore the world of engineering and entrepreneurship. Each Shad Valley group has 50 students who have demonstrated: (a) high academic achievement, especially in math and science, (b) creativity, (c) initiative and drive, and (d) good interpersonal skills. In 1996 Shad Valley programs ran at Acadia and Carleton University, the Universities of British Columbia, Calgary, New Brunswick, and Waterloo, and the Université de Sherbrooke. High school science teachers should have program details and application forms. The application deadline is in December for the coming summer.

Study in Oxford and/or France with Peel Board of Education, Community Education, Summer Programs, 160 Traders Blvd. E., #114, Mississauga, Ontario L4Z 3K7. (905) 568-1080, #230, fax (905) 568-4690, Internet http://www.comed.on.ca/ and

Blyth & Company Travel, Summer Programs, 13 Hazelton Ave., Toronto, Ontario, M5R 2E1. 1-800-387-1387, 1-800-964-3416 (Ontario), fax (416) 964-3416 - Students can take credit courses in English literature, creative writing, media studies, business, art history, world issues and other topics at Oxford University in the United Kingdom, courses in the French language or photography in the south of France, or combine studies in both England and France.

U.S. Space and Rocket Center Space Academy, 1 Tranquility Base, Huntsville, Alabama U.S.A. 35807-7015. 1-800-63-SPACE - These programs give students the opportunity to work with NASA equipment, and learn about scientific, engineering and aviation aspects of the U.S. Space Program. Aviation Challenge is a five-day program adapted from the U.S. Navy fighter-pilot training program. Students fly simulated missions in flight simulators and learn the basics of aviation. U.S. Space Academy, Level II, emphasizes the academic foundation of aerospace and other high-tech careers. Students train in a variety of U.S. Space and Rocket Center equipment, including a Space Station module. Participants elect a technology, engineering or aerospace track as a focus to their activities during the eight-day program.

TAKING A GRADE 13 YEAR BEFORE UNIVERSITY

For a variety of reasons, you may want to take a Grade 13 year or wait a year after Grade 12 before going to university. If you'd like to take a Grade 13 year, many public, separate and independent schools in Ontario offer OAC/Grade 13 courses. You can get school listings from the Ontario Ministry of Education or the Canadian Association of Independent Schools [(416) 488-6424].

If you aren't interested in Grade 13, but want to wait for a year after grade 12 before attending university, there are possibilities in addition to work or independent travel. International options include the following organized opportunities available for university-age students. These programs can be expensive, but many offer scholarships and financial aid to qualified participants.

AFS Interculture Canada, 1231 St. Catherine Street West, Suite 505, Montreal, Quebec H3G 1P5. (514) 288-3282, 1-800-361-7248 (Eastern Canada), 1-800-361-1879 (Western Canada and Newfoundland) -

AFS organizes international exchanges that give students the opportunity to live with host families and attend school in another country for a full year or semester. Ten or twelve-month exchanges can be arranged for Australia, New Zealand, Argentina, Bolivia, Brazil, Chile, Costa Rica, Ecuador, Japan and Thailand; six month exchanges go to Costa Rica, Argentina and other countries.

Canadian College Italy, 59 Macamo Ct., Maple, Ontario L6A 1G1. (905) 508-7108, 1-800-422-0548, fax (905) 508-5480, e-mail staff@cci.lanciano.ch.it, Internet http://web.idirect.com/~cci/ - Canadian College Italy in Lanciano, Italy is a co-ed school that stresses academic excellence, and a traditional academic curriculum. School highlights include state-of-the-art science facilities, small classes, and supervised travel in Italy and throughout Europe.

EF International Language Schools, 60 Bloor Street West, Suite 405, Toronto, Ontario M4W 3B8. (416) 323-0330, 1-800-387-1463, fax (416) 927-8664 - Nine month language courses are offered in Spain, Italy, France and Germany with options for differing levels of instruction intensity. Students can elect to live with local families.

Katimavik, 2065 Rue Parthenais, Suite 405, Montreal, Quebec H2K 3T1. (514) 525-1503, toll free 1-888-525-1503, fax (514) 525-1953 - Katimavik was founded in 1976 by the federal government to provide work experience for Canadian youth. It was discontinued for several years, but reinstated in 1995. Katimavik is a seven and a half month program for Canadians between the ages of 17 and 21. Participants live in groups, work in three different regions of Canada on non-profit projects, and hone their skills in a second language. (e.g., French or English)

Lycée canadien en France, 13 Hazelton Avenue, Toronto, Ontario M5R 2E1. (416) 926-0828, 1-800-387-5603 (Ontario), 1-800-387-1387, fax (416) 964-3416 - The Lycée has a rigorous academic focus, but also prepares students to be self-motivated independent thinkers who are ready for the demands of university life. Students live at the school or with carefully selected families in nearby villages.

Neuchâtel Junior College, 330 Bay Street, Toronto, Ontario M5H 2S8. (416) 368-8169, 1-800-263-2923, e-mail info@neuchatel.org - Neuchâtel Junior College, located in the historic city of Neuchâtel, Switzerland, is a long-established school which offers an academically stimulating, culturally rich program. The school is co-ed. Students have the opportunity for extensive European travel and residency in French-speaking homes.

A two year opportunity is provided by:

United World Colleges, London House, Mecklenburgh Square, London, United Kingdom WC1N 2AB. (44 171) 833 2626, fax (44 171) 837 3102, e-mail uwcio@gn.apc.org, Internet http://owlnet.rice.edu/~walkerb/uwc/uwchome/html/ - The United World Colleges are a group of nine related schools located throughout the world. Students, aged 16 to 19, come to the Colleges from around the world to study and learn in an environment of peace, cooperation, and personal challenge. All students stay two years and study for the International Baccalaureate exams. Atlantic College is located in Wales, Lester B. Pearson College in Canada, Armand Hammer College in the United States, Adriatic College in Italy, Waterford-Kamhlaba College in Swaziland, UWC of South East Asia in Singapore, Simon Bolivar College in Venezuela, Li Po Chum College in Hong Kong, and Red Cross Nordic College in Norway.

GOING TO UNIVERSITY

A Final Thought

Preparing to go to university can seem like a daunting exercise if you don't know the questions to ask or where to find the information you need to make an informed decision. Yet, when you have marshaled all the information you need, the decision can be easy and the whole process can give you a good start on the next part of your life. Marshaling the information is important.

I hope this guide has helped you. Good luck with your search and with your university studies!

GOING TO UNIVERSITY

Index

A

Aboriginal students 5, 55
Acadia University 4, 5, 33
ACT 15, 16, 37, 74, 75, 76
admission requirements 12, 14, 68-76
    American 74-76
    Canadian 69-71
advanced placement (AP) 69
AFS Interculture Canada 95, 98
Alberta, University of 45, 53, 61
American schools 13, 14, 15, 36-41
application deadlines 15, 15, 16
    American 72
    Canadian 70
application process 14, 45, 48, 49
    American 71-75
    Canadian 68-71
Apply software 39, 72
Arizona, University of 46
Art Student's College Guide (US) 40
Athabasca University 83
athletic scholarships 57-58
Auburn University (US) 72

Augustana University College 5
average students, (US) guide for 41

B

Barron's Guide to the Best, Most Popular, and Most Exciting Colleges (US) 37
Barron's Guide to the Most Prestigious Colleges (US) 37
benefits of a university education 9
Best College for You (US) 39, 49, 72
Bill Mason Memorial Scholarship 54
Brandon University 5
Brescia College 79
British Columbia Open University 83
British Columbia, scholarships 54
British Columbia, University of 4-5, 28, 45, 61
Bryn Mawr College (US) 45
bursary 6, 53

C

(100) Colleges Where Average Students Can Excel (US) 41
Calgary, University of 4, 61
Campion College 79
campus visits 14, 15, 27, 48, 60-66
Canada Student Loans 55
Canadian Association of Independent Schools 98
Canadian College Italy 99
Canadian Scholarships on File 54-55
career options 13, 18-20
Carleton College Summer Writing Program 95
Carleton University 61
CD-ROMs 48-49, 54
Choices 19
co-op programs 53
College Admissions (US) 73
College Applications and Essays (US) 73
College Prospects of America (CPOA) 57-58
College Scholarships and Financial Aid (US) 56
Colleges that Change Lives (US) 41
colleges within Canadian universities 62, 78-80
commuter campuses 4-5
Complete Guide to Canadian Universities 33
Conrad Grebel College 80
Cornell University (US) 45
cost, opportunity 6
costs of a university education 6-9
Cracking the SAT & PSAT 73
culture, campus 3-6, 22

D

Dalhousie University 61, 79
Deep River Science Academy 95
distance education 82-83
Do What You Are 20

E

e-mail 44, 45, 46, 62, 72
early admission decisions (US) 72
EF International Language Schools 96, 99
equestrian studies 38

F

Financial Aid Need Estimator (US) 56
financial aid
    American 16, 49
    Canadian 15, 53-55
Fiske Guide to Colleges (US) 37
fit, between student and school 3, 80, 87
France, summer programs in 96, 97

G

Georgetown University 72
Get Yourself a College Sports Scholarship (US) 58
Getting Into College (US) 49
Globe and Mail 20
Gourman Report 34, 40
Grade 9 13, 72
Grade 10 12, 13, 72, 74
Grade 11 13, 69, 72, 74
Grade 12 12, 13, 14, 69, 70, 72, 74
Grade 13 98-100
grants 53
Guelph, University of 61

H

Harvard University (US) 45, 72
Harvard University Summer School 96
Historically Black Colleges and Universities (US) 41
home pages 44-46, 70
How to Get Into College (US) 39
Howell, Michael 55
Huron College 3, 79

Innis College 79
International Baccalaureate program 100
Internet information 27, 34, 44-46, 55, 58, 70, 72, 82, 83
interviewing a school 62-66

K

Kaplan Educational Centers 39, 73
Katimavik 99
King's College (Dalhousie) 79
King's College (Western Ontario) 79

L

learning disabled students, guide for 40
Lester B. Pearson College 46, 100
loans 53
Lovejoy's College Guide (US) 38
Lovejoy's College Guide for the Learning Disabled (US) 40
Luther College 79
Lycée canadien en France 99

M

Maclean's Guide to Universities 33
Maclean's viii, ix, 33, 71
Manitoba, University of 5, 28, 61, 79, 83
Massachusetts Institute of Technology (MIT) (US) 72
McGill University 5, 28, 45, 61
McMaster University 5
Merit Program (US) 57
Merit Scholarships® (US) 57
Michigan, University of (US) 45, 72
Middlebury College (US) 45
Money magazine (US) 39
Montreal, University of 61
Mount Allison University 28, 61
Mount St. Vincent University 61
Myers-Briggs Type Indicator® 14, 19, 20

N

National Merit Scholarships (US) 57, 74
Neuchâtel Junior College 100
New Brunswick, University of 45, 61
New College 79

INDEX

Newsweek 39
Northern British Columbia, University of 5
Northwestern University (US) 72
Notre Dame University (US) 72O

O

Ohio State University (US) 72
Open University 83
open admissions policy 69
Operation Catapult 96
opportunity cost 6
Ottawa, University of 61
Oxford University, study at 97

P

Parent's Guide 46, 55
part-time students 55
peace studies 38, 100
Peel Board of Education summer programs 97
Performing Arts Major's College Guide (US) 40
Peterson's Four Year Colleges (US) 38, 56
Peterson's Guide to New England Colleges (US) 38

Please Understand Me 20
Prince Edward Island, University of 45
Princeton Review 39, 49, 72, 73
Princeton Review's Student Access Guide to the Best Colleges (US) 38
PSAT 13, 14, 57, 74, 76
PSAT/NMSQT 57, 74

Q

Queen's University 4-5, 28, 45, 61
questionnaire, school selection 23-27

R

Redeemer College 5
residential campuses 4-5
Royal Roads University 5
room and board costs 6, 8, 37
Real Guide to Canadian Universities 33
Reed College (US) 46
rankings of schools viii, 33, 34, 39, 40
Regina, University of 45, 61, 79
Resume, Your First 70

Rutgers University (US) 72
Renison College 80
rolling admissions policy 72

S

St. Andrew's College 79
St. Boniface, Collège universitaire de 79
St. Francis Xavier University 5
St. Jerome's College 79
St. John's College 3, 54, 79
St. Mary's University 61
St. Michael's College 79
St. Paul's College (Manitoba) 79
St. Paul's College (Waterloo) 80
St. Thomas More College 79
St. Thomas University 61
Saskatchewan Indian Federated College 79
Saskatchewan, University of 5, 61, 79
SAT I 13, 14, 15, 16, 72, 74-76
SAT II 13, 14, 15, 72, 75
Scholarship Search Software (US) 56
scholarships 8, 14, 48, 52-58, 67
    American 56-57
    Canadian 52-55, 70

School Finder CD-ROM 48-49
school selection questionnaire 23-27, 49
Sea Education Association 97
selective admissions policies 4, 69, 73, 87
Senior I 13
Senior II 12, 13
Senior III 13
Senior IV 12, 13, 14
Shad Valley Summer Program 97
Simon Fraser University 61
Space Academy, U.S. Space and Rocket Center 98
standardized tests 49, 73-76
Stanford University (US) 46
Strong Interest Inventory TM 14, 19
summer educational opportunities 94-98

T

Terry Fox Scholarship 54
Time magazine 39, 49, 72
Toronto, University of 5, 45, 61, 79
Transfer Student's Guide to Changing Colleges (US) 41
transition to university, dealing with 87-88

Trent University 28, 45
Trinity College 79
tuition 6, 8, 37

U

U.S. News and World Report 39, 49
U.S. News and World Report Exclusive Rankings of the Best Colleges (US) 39
U.S. Space and Rocket Center Space Academy 98
United World Colleges 46, 100
Université d' Ottawa 61
Université de Montréal 61
University College (Manitoba) 79
University College (Toronto) 79
University of California-Berkeley (US) 72
University of California-Davis (US) 46

V

Victoria College 79
Victoria, University of 61
visits to universities 14

W

Waterloo, University of 54, 61, 71, 79, 83
Western Ontario, University of 3, 53, 61, 79
Wilfrid Laurier University 61
Winning Scholarships 55
Winnipeg, University of 28, 61
Women's Colleges (US) 40
Woodsworth College 79
work-study arrangements 53

Y

York University 33, 61
Your Best College Buys Now (US) 39